PASSIVE INCOME IDEAS

Make Money Online Through E-Commerce, Dropshipping, Social Media Marketing, Blogging, Affiliate Marketing, Retail Arbitrage and More

Rachel Smith

TABLE OF CONTENTS

CHAPTER 1
Passive Income Basics

Passive Income is the earning resulting from a source in which the person is not working actively. In other words, we can describe it as the cash flow coming to a person without making any effort to obtain it. Historically, it has been divided into two categories by the experts which are rental income or limited partnership in a business. The passive income also comes under the radar of government taxes.

Understanding Passive Income

There are generally three legal forms of income: active income, passive income, or portfolio income. The first two forms are a traditional source of income in which the person puts his/her effort to get the return in the form of cash flows. However, the recently emerged term passive income, relates to the scenario where the person is earning from a source or business in spite of doing almost no work. This means that you are generating income while you are on a trip with your family on an island or sleeping in your bed. The income cash flow does not get affected by the fact whether you are putting the focus on it on a daily basis. However, don't get confused by these statements that it requires no effort to create passive revenue for you. The passive income is actually a scenario in which you first have to set up a revenue stream that benefits you in the long term.

The sources of income can vary from usual business ideas or transforming your hobbies or daily activities into the revenue source. For example, if you are a video game lover, there is a possibility of earning money by just playing games. For this, you just need to create an account on YouTube with gaming videos. After that, just monetized this YouTube account with advertisements ranging from video to banner ads. Many of the people with a larger YouTube audience have been offered a partnership by YouTube. One can analyze that this income source can be generated without making any such investment. Due to these reasons, experienced passive income earners recommend hobbies to be the best place to start with.

The traditional passive income sources which exist for a number of years turn out to be rental, trading, and sleeping partnerships. The public is earning passive income money from ages through the concept of giving property on rent. Similarly, the investment in the stock market is another source of passive income that has been traditionally utilized. However, with the advent of the technology world, passive income sources have increased dramatically. People with simple qualifications are earning a handsome livelihood through these sources. The technology world is offering social media, e-commerce, and web platforms to the public for setting up revenue streams that require no effort.

Developing the Positive Mindset

The process of creating income for yourself results in financial independence, which is the first priority of most of the people in the world. One has to put some initial efforts for the setup or wait for some time to save money for investing in the passive income business, such as rental property. However, once you start the process, then it has no further complexities in growing up. The issue for most people arises is initial effort and myths regarding passive income earnings. Many people get into this trap and do not indulge in passive income business. However, if you want to earn money in a passive way, then you need to realize that the positive mindset regarding the process is essential.

According to Hellen Keller,

"Keep your face to the sunshine, and you cannot see a shadow."
The optimism regarding future works is always necessary to succeed in your life. Therefore, avoid any negative thoughts in your mindset and get positive results through the different passive income ideas available in the market. In the era of technology, passive income can be earned from the number of platforms by common users. One just requires the much-needed motivation and positive mindset to start earning passive income.

It Primarily Starts With Passions

Money making is the primary aim of most of the people planning for new ideas around the world. How to earn it in a quick, easy, and simple way without making much effort and spending time is a top priority in our daily thoughts. The main goal is to live with passion with passive income generation that is stable enough to avoid any financial concerns. But, how is that possible for a common man? Ordinary people keep working in a field or profession that they have no interest in. Passion only comes to their profession until they start getting financial advantages from it. In contrast, if we read the case studies of successful people, the common thing we found is the start doing passionate things and then plan on how to make money out of them. In other words,
"Do what you love, and then you won't have to work again in your life."
One just needs to believe in the fact that it is possible to get financial gain from his/her passion. You just have to figure out what your passions are and then plan for them to earn income out of them. The best possible

choice is to start working on your passion part-time. The reason is that it is not smart for a person to leave the current job or business as it can prove to be financially disastrous. Therefore, dedicate some part of the day to your passion and then start planning and developing it to a profitable venture.

It Takes More Than Just Passion

Passion is the most exciting thing while planning for your business idea. However, do not get blind from your enthusiasm to work in a specific field. Everyone first questions whether he/she is willing to work hard in its field of passion and whether there is a market space available for you or not. Moreover, make sure you have the required skills to present something professional to the public.

Passive income is an exciting business strategy, especially for those who are unable to work for their side business due to daily routine activities. The consistent cash flow in your account without any particular effort can make your lifestyle better in many ways. However, there must be careful planning and selection of suitable business ideas to fulfill your aim of earning passive income in modern days. In the upcoming chapters, we will provide you top trending and useful business ideas that will enable you to generate profits passively.

Why With the Formula S.M.A.R.T.

Every business in the market has set a particular goal to achieve in the future in order to achieve larger objectives. Although every entrepreneur has the importance of business goals in his or her mind, there are still plenty of examples where the companies failed due to a lack of focused goals. Small business owners, most of the time, make a mistake that they keep the priority of getting "more business" regarding their future plans. SMART goal setting is a valuable strategy in every business, especially in our case, where we are looking to set up a passive income stream. You should understand the SMART goal setting strategy in order to apply it for your business where you are looking to generate passive income.

The SMART acronym contains five elements in their domain which are as follows:

- Specific
- Measurable
- Achievable
- Relevant
- Time-based goals.

A SMART strategy is a simple tool that businessmen use to set their future goals for their companies. The elements of this strategy are discussed in detail below.

5.1. Specific

The goals must be well-defined and specific in nature. Otherwise, your workforce will not be able to focus, and as a business owner, your motivation level can go down. For example, If you set a goal "Obtain 1 Billion USD worth clients located in Newyork construction market," then it can be termed as specific. As opposed to this, if your business goal is " Get more business," then it cannot be called as well-defined and focused. The reason is when you have focused a goal; then it acts like a magnet pulls and your resources towards it. Unspecific goals do not have that magnet pull in their domain. The SMART business goal setting should address the following questions to make it specific in nature.

- What is the business looking to achieve?
- What is the significance of the goal?
- Who are the stakeholders and involved in it?
- What is the location of the business and goal?
- What are the specifications of the resources involved in the process?

5.2. Measurable

It is very important that your goals are measurable in nature, which will enable you to track the progress and performance in order to achieve them. The assessment of progress helps you to complete the tasks on set deadlines, stay motivated, and increase excitement related to the achievement of goals. Therefore, it is safer to say that any goal that has no measurable outcome then is comparable to a sports tournament where there is no points table. Hence, when you are setting goals for the business, make sure you place concrete numbers to it for the purpose of tracking. Moreover, to stay focused on the achievement of the goals, place a goal whiteboard in your office to keep yourself and the workers motivated for achieving this target.

5.3. Attainable

Many businesses fail due to setting unrealistic goals that are beyond reach. Similarly, when you are looking for a passive income business, then keep it in mind that you cannot earn millions overnight. Therefore, dream big and conceptualize it but place one foot in the reality field to set an achievable goal. You must keep two factors in mind while setting a goal for your business,

- How will I achieve this goal?
- Is the goal attainable in reality, keeping all the constraints involved in it?

The goal must stretch your skills and capacities. However, it should still be in the possible range. Moreover, you must review the previously missed opportunities to successfully attain it in the future.

5.4. Relevant

This aspect of the SMART goal setting ensures that the goal you are aiming for is well-aligned with the other relevant targets and goals. Moreover, the goal you set is based on the trending market conditions and are relevant to the business climate. As a business owner, you should target growth in revenue, but what about the strong recession period in the market. Similarly, while setting a passive income stream, you must choose the future goals according to the market value of the business idea you have selected for it. Furthermore, to ensure the relevance of the goal, do an analysis of the capabilities and resources you have under the belt to achieve it.

5.5 Time-based Goals

Business goals and the target cannot be settled completely until you do not assign any time-frame or deadline to it. For example, if you are looking to attain five more clients, then you must set a deadline for it, such as in the next three months, from April to June 2019. Every goal requires a target date or time so that you make this long-term goal priority over the daily routine activities. The time factor should also be critical in setting a goal for passive income, whether it is to increase income, clients, or quality.

Once you have settled down the goals for business according to SMART criteria, then divide them into different tasks to attain them. The SMART criteria also have critical importance while implementing any passive income business model. It helps you to achieve the major aim behind your initiative of doing side business for generating cash flow into your account with any particular effort. The passive income goals also involve some other factors apart from SMART criteria. You need to address these factors for a successful business venture.

- Plan what is your total budget to set up the income stream and how much you are looking to spend each month in the starting days of the passive income business?

- What are your time-based expectations related to the passive income stream? Analyze how much time you want this income stream to provide you cash flow passively?
- What is the deadline to earn a profit for the first time through this passive income stream?

CHAPTER 2
Kindle Publishing

Kindle Publishing is offering a platform to everyone to set up a passive income stream where 500-5000 monthly dollars can be earned with little work involved. The secret behind this is the right strategy, initial hard work, and patience. With Kindle Publishing, everyone can earn money through publishing e-books and reach millions of people looking to read books online. The publishing e-book is a simple and cheap process that enables you to start generating revenue within 24 hours. The best thing about the Kindle Publishing platform is that it offers book owners to keep control of their rights with self-desired pricing. Moreover, the writers of the book can make changes to it at any time.

According to market research, Amazon has been the top e-retailer company in the USA. As a newbie in the online business world, Kindle Publishing is the best platform for you. It offers passive income without placing a lot of effort and initial financial investment. If we make a comparison of Kindle Publishing to other passive income sources, then it turns out to be the least complex out of them. However, you need the right strategy and step by step approach to get yourself a reliable source of income. The step by step guide to earning passive income through Kindle Publishing is present below;

Find a Niche or Market

Just before starting your work on the e-book, do some research to target the right market to publish the book. It is commonly observed that people with great ideas or topics are not able to sell their books on the Amazon platform. The reason behind this scenario is that it is not only the good content that makes your product go on the top of the list in best sellers. Market research can gap analysis is also very significant to getting yourself earned through Kindle Publishing.

Keyword Research

The first step is to find out the right keywords to market your book. The aim should be to research what words or keywords people are typing to search for books related to a specific topic. Start with doing analysis on what's hot in the market and then tailor your book according to the demand. The book must be optimized with the right keywords so that when someone searches on Amazon, your book appears to be in the suggested list.

Create a Winning Title and Cover

Have you ever heard the phrase "Never Judge a book by its cover"? If you do, then please ignore it as this theory does not apply in the case of Kindle Publishing. To maximize your sales, it is critical to creating an attractive cover page with a title. The focus should be to grab the attention of the client so that he/she gives a thought about purchasing your book. They must develop anxiety in the mind to read what's inside your book. For this, it isn't necessary to do all the work by you. There are a number of freelance workers available on websites such as Fiver, where you can get a creative design for a book and cover page at cheap rates.

Create Quality Content

The ultimate goal while writing the book must be to produce content that makes your audience think that they have gained some excellent knowledge from it. The quality content leads to positive reviews from the audience, which is essential for boosting the sale. However, do not get disappointed by the negative feedback in starting days as you get to improve with the time in every field.

Kindle Direct Publishing Account

After doing all the work related to the book, now it's time to set up your account on the Kindle Publishing platform. For this, some easy steps are required to be completed by you. Moving on, upload the book and set the price you want to sell it for. The process of clarification works quickly in Kindle Publishing. Once you click on the "Publish" button, the books get available status within 24-48 hours.

Marketing of the Book

Publishing of the book on Amazon is just the beginning of your work. In order to attract the audience, a strong marketing campaign is required. At Amazon, if anyone wants to be a successful seller, he/she needs to master marketing techniques according to modern standards. Experts in the marketing field recommend the following ideas to the newcomers to market their book on Kindle Publishing.

1. Do research on the right keywords to be in the list of subjects people are searching for.
2. Start a Pay Per Click campaign for your book. This will cost you money charged by Google and Amazon.
3. Promote your book on social media platforms such as Facebook or Twitter.

In the end, Kindle Publishing may seem to be easy for you; however, it requires the initial hard work to make your book a brand. Get yourself hard work at the start and earn Passive income for a long while through Kindle Publishing.

CHAPTER 3
Real Estate Investing

Real Estate Investment is a traditional business to start earning passive income. It is very popular among the common public to own the rental properties for getting reliable income. The real estate industry has been the most beneficial according to the studies to generate a passive income stream for anyone. However, just like all other businesses, everyone is advised to not start the work in a hurry and do some proper research before taking any initiative.

Why Invest in Real Estate?

Real estate provides a number of reasons to invest in it. Apart from the passive income source, it is ideal for you to get the cash flow even after retirement. Moreover, for younger people, it boosts the entrepreneurial spirit in their minds. The real estate benefits the owners due to its status as a perfect hedge for inflation. When the price level goes up, the rent automatically rises, which increases the revenue of the owners. Overall, it is recommended to be one of the safest investments in the market. Getting your property on rent is a commonly utilized method for earning passive income through real estate, but the real estate market has some other great opportunities too for you under its belt.

Real Estate Investment Trust

Real Estate Investment Trust provides the opportunity to the public to invest in commercial real estate properties without going physically for the purchase of the property. The publicly traded REITS are available for investment in national security and stock exchanges. The investment can be made by purchasing public-traded REIT through the stock exchange. In contrast, the market also has non traded public REITs for investment purposes. They are beneficial for investment because they are protected from market volatility.

Realty Mogul

For people looking to invest in real estate just by sitting at home, realty mogul is an ideal online market platform for them. It is recommended as the crowdfunding real estate opportunity where the investment and sponsors collaborate for making an investment in real estate. Reality Moguls offers stocks in one of its Limited Liability to the investors. The LLC then makes an investment in another LLC in the market which holds title to the property. However, the notable thing is that they offer a minimum investment of 1000 dollars.

Mobile Home Parks

The ongoing economic stress in the financial world has increased the demand for mobile homes and land utilized for this. The owner of the mobile home parks basically owns the land. The revenue source is the rent it takes from the people that choose to locate their homes on its land. As a new entry into this field, one has the option to go for a partnership with experienced mobile home park investors easily. However, this investment requires large funding for creating the setup.

Tax Lien Certificates

Whenever a home or property owner fails to submit its taxes, the state departments issue tax lien certificates on that property. The basic purpose of the tax lien certificate is to make a record that the related property owes this amount of tax to the state. These tax lien certificates are available to purchase through the auction process. The property owners have to pay the amount of tax to the tax liens with interest rates. This makes it a reliable passive income source for investors.

Hard Money Loans

In this method or idea, the investor becomes a part-time banking channel in which provides loans to people with the real-estate property as collateral. It includes minimum risk as in case if any problem occurs, investors can easily sell the property to get its money back. However, the hard money loans should be given with proper background study regarding the worth of property and legality of ownership claims.

Steps for Real Estate Investing

In the previous section, we recommend the ideas or ways to earn passive income through real estate. Moving on, this section will provide you a 5 step plan to get started with real estate passive income.

1. Identify your Financial Position
Real estate requires a strong investment and financial position in its initial phase. If your financial position is not strong, then it's best for you to do some savings at a fast rate. Without the proper budget, it will be hard for you to grab the market to earn a constant income. The basics of real estate investment are quite similar to that of climbing up a mountain.

In other words, the more you save, the more likely you are going to reach the mountain.

2. Choose a Strategy
There are a number of wealth strategies available on the internet and the market. According to your financial position, make use of them, which provides you guidelines related to the wealth stage such as survival or stability, saving, and growth. In each phase of your business, there should also be a backup strategy in place for you.

3. Target Market
The market analysis is critical for achieving positive results in any field. We have recommended you five categories to invest in real estate other than the traditional model of rental properties. Do an evaluation and research which market or field suits you in terms of financial position, location, and mindset.

4. Raise Cash
Real estate investment is a field where you have the option to utilize money from other sources to grow in the market. Similarly, for setting up a passive income stream, you should use different sources to generate cash and funds for investing and reserves. The best possible option is to take loans from private lenders or banking channels.

5. Create a Plan
Planning all stages of your initial real estate investment is necessary for success. First of all, you have to choose the real estate industry and then make your investment plan in all possible situations. Moving on, work on how to accelerate the growth strategy, and plan the exit option from the business.

Real Estate Investment has been used as the source of passive income for centuries. In this traditional model of passive income, there are new options in this era of technology. However, the new entrants must know that this can be the riskiest business option if you haven't done proper planning in advance.

CHAPTER 4

Amazon Fba

You must have heard about the e-commerce giant Amazon once in your life. However, if not, then you must know that it is an online platform that allows us to order products related to almost anything virtually and delivers us within a few days at our desired location. But, there exists a category of Amazon, which surely few of us are familiar with: Amazon FBA (fulfilled by Amazon). It is a platform for online sellers where they can place their products in Amazon fulfillment centers. Amazon provides the services of packing, packing, and shipping on behalf of these sellers to the customers. All you have to do is to relax at home and earn passive income with the fact that your products are sold to people all around the world.

Benefits of FBA

When you list your products in the warehouse of Amazon, then it takes the whole responsibility off the next process. What can be more passive about this business? Moreover, the most attractive and comfortable thing Amazon FBA does is that it provides the customer service even after delivering the product. Once your product is running, then the workload on you gets very low with the arrival of regular income to your account. You just have to restock the products in the inventory of Amazon FBA when all of the previous listings are sold out. Apart from this, Amazon FBA offers you some other benefits too.

> 1.1. FBA items and products appear on the top of search results. Customers usually like to purchase the stuff that is recommended to them. Moreover, the products of FBA are also food to be present in the buy box more than the other listings.
> 1.2. The costs spent on delivering the items on the location of customers are included in the fees you pay to Amazon FBA.
> 1.3. You have the chance to be eligible for Amazon Prime member benefits, which have the option of free delivery. Customers are observed to be attracted to these offers.

The Formula for Passive Income at Amazon FBA.

From the initial introductory paragraph and benefits section, you can have an idea about the formula of earning passive income at FBA. It requires 3 steps by you.

2.1. Find the items or products you have the chance to earn profit from.

2.2. Source and ship them to the Amazon warehouse for the next work.

2.3. Sit at home and earn money without any further effort.

Cost to Start Selling

Hopefully, this isn't a surprise for you at all. For selling products through Amazon FBA, you have to spend some starting costs in different stages. The main cost will be spent on cracking a deal for physical inventory. Moreover, shipping costs for delivering products to Amazon and then fees for shipment service to acquire FBA service is also required. Besides these main costs, a seller is required to pay the cost for the following things.

· Referral fees by the Amazon
· Storage fees for the warehouse provided by Amazon
· Subscription costs

You should do the calculation of the overall costs after choosing the product related to shipment and storage. The total budget spent depends upon your plan; however, since you are new to the business, therefore, it is recommended to start with the MVP model. This model means to provide a minimum viable product to the customers for getting experience.

FBA Process

Amazon provides you the full responsibility after you have placed your stock in and complete all the legal requirements. The FBA process is simple enough to be used by everyone to generate passive income for themselves. Every seller has to go through the following stages at Amazon FBA.

1. Research the Product

This stage involves thorough study of the Amazon virtual market. The aim is to get information about the demand for specific products in the market. The focus should be upon making a collection of options to choose the product which you can earn profit from. It would be great if you can locate the item where demand is high, but the competition level is not tough so that you can have the first-mover advantage.

2. Choose the Right product

This is the most critical stage where you need to attain a profitable product through a reliable source. Take a look at what methods are available for you to complete this stage.

2.1.WholeSalers

It is sometimes referred to be the product-first approach. You can bargain products with wholesalers and compare them to the price available on Amazon by the other sellers. The reduced wholesale value allows you to advertise products at lower rates to attract customers. It is potentially the best method to find a profitable product for Amazon FBA.

2.2. Suppliers

Although this method requires some extra effort from the seller, if done in the right way, then it can generate a lot of profit. The products can be found at cheaper rates leaving you a margin to manage the profits and discount offers to the customers. Moreover, for maximizing profits, products can be sold as private labels. This means you can sell them as your own brand. However, you have to do repackaging and labeling to sell it as your own product.

3. Sign Up at Amazon FBA

Alright, you have chosen the product and sourcing method, now it's time to get sign up at FBA. It requires details related to banking, subscription, and name of your company. Keep in mind that Amazon will ask you to provide verification for these details. The display name has critical importance as you must choose the name in which the customers can relate to your product or at least cannot get offended by it.

4. Adding Products to Inventory

Before the arrival of all products from suppliers, add them to your inventory at FBA. It can be done online through your seller account.

- Select "Add Product" from the inventory page.
- Choose the product category, style, and color. First, select the product from
- UPC or ISBN number. In case you are bringing a new product, then click on the button "Not in Amazon Catalogue" and then follow the next instructions to add it.
- Click on save and finish button on the last page to complete the process
- Repeat the process for all the products you are looking to add one by one.

5. Inventory Placement Options

The Amazon FBA account lets you edit the settings according to your choice related to the products. At the start, the most critical setting is inventory placement. For this, the seller has two choices in the options list.

5.1. Distributed Inventory Placement

In this setting, you have to send products to several FBA warehouses for the further process. It is default settings but certainly not in favor of sellers. This will require you to deliver the products by yourself to different warehouses separately. This means that you have to put extra effort into delivering the product as well as the overhead cost for shipping the products to different warehouses.

5.2. Inventory Placement Option

Here, you will send your products to a single warehouse, and then Amazon will take care of further delivery to other units. However, there is a small fee of $0.30 per 1 lb. product for this activity.

6. Marketing and Promotion

Is there any business in the world without marketing? Well, definitely, "No." Similarly, there is a strong marketing campaign required for your products on Amazon FBA. You can utilize social media and Pay per click offered by search engines. Once your products get listings, then it is simple for you to relax at home without making any hard effort to boost up the sales. The noticeable point is you require financing for the pay-per-click campaign and for social media tools for reaching a larger audience.

In the end, Amazon FBA is no quick rich scheme for you, but the initial work can pay you off in terms of earning passive income. The process has no complexities with just a few simple steps to put your steps in the worldwide market.

Market Via Facebook Ads

The proper ad campaign structure is crucial for any business, small or large, and any brand, whether that brand supports a single product or many products. With a well-formed, thoughtfully-designed ad campaign, your company could see an increase in website or social media traffic, an increase in profits, improved brand recognition, and so much more! An effective campaign structure is the first step in a successful ad campaign, as it will help you to set specific goals for specific campaigns, measure the results of those campaigns, discover which campaigns are working and which are not, and allocate your budget in the most effective way possible.

It will also help you to create multiple ad sets for multiple audiences so that you can determine who is most likely to generate business for your company or brand. Through variations in image, text, links, and videos, a properly structured campaign will even allow you to see what types of ads are having the biggest impact on your audience.

A Facebook ad campaign has three levels. At the top is the Campaign, then the Ad Set, and then the Ad itself. At the campaign level, you will choose an objective or goal like "Increase Sales" or "Increase Total Likes for my Business Facebook Page." At the Ad Set level, you will set your budget, your schedule, your target audience, and your ad placement.

Once you have chosen the parameters of your ad set, you will design your ad or multiple ads to be run with the same ad set. Your ad set may contain one or more ads, and the ads must be individual creations that contain text, video, images, and/or links. Your ad set is what will attract attention to your business or brand and will help you achieve both your short-term and long-term goals.

Step one

The first step towards creating an effective ad campaign structure is to set firm and clear goals, and then to allocate each goal to an individual campaign. Then, every ad set and ad will be oriented towards your chosen objectives - no matter how big or small, how long-term, or how short term. For example, your objective may be something like increasing the number of installs your app has, increasing overall traffic to your website, increasing sales of a particular item, or simply to generate more "Likes" for your Facebook business page.

Tip #1: Limit one objective per advertisement; that way, you can tailor your audience and budget to achieve maximum value from your ad campaign.

Tip #2: Get creative! If your objective is to increase Page Likes, consider designing an ad that offers a 10% discount code to anyone who Likes and Follows your business Facebook page. While this would work well for increasing Facebook Page Likes, offering 10% off for a Facebook Like may not generate more website traffic, since your website is not directly involved. This is why we recommend limiting your objectives to one objective per ad.

Step two

The second step is to allocate your ad sets to the audiences you most want to target. One ad set might be aimed at Men, age 18 to 24, while another ad set might aim at Women, age 18 to 24. It is important to allocate different ad sets to different audiences so that your ad sets do not end up competing with one other. It is also important to keep your target audience in mind when designing each ad set. Men may be more likely to stop and look at an ad that includes a scantily-clad model in it, but most women will probably scroll right past - or worse, they may block the ad.

When you allocate your audience, you will also be at the point in ad set design where you will get to determine how to allocate your budget and the different aspects of budgeting you will need to keep in mind. The first two aspects of budgeting to consider are Daily Budget and Lifetime Budget.

• Daily Budget: the amount you are willing to spend on an ad set per day.
• Lifetime Budget: the amount you are willing to spend on an ad set in total.

Once your budget has been set, the Facebook Ads Manager will spread your Lifetime Budget out over the entire length of your ad campaign. Doing so may cause your Daily Budget to decrease, but Facebook Ads Manager will never exceed the Daily Budget you originally set. This ensures that Facebook Ads Manager never goes "over-budget" on any aspect of your campaign and that you never spend more money than you are willing to spend on an ad campaign.

Tip: Set a cap on your expenditures, track how much money you have spent using Facebook's spend meters, and measure your campaign's performance using the ads reporting tab in the Facebook Ads Manager.

Tip: Avoid changing your budget type mid-campaign. Doing so will reset your budget, and this may alter the ad analysis provided by Facebook Ads manager. Also, you can use the Audience Insight feature in Ads Manager to help with your target selection.

Step three

The third step is to bid for your various objectives. For example, let us say that your chosen objective was to direct traffic to your website. In that case, Facebook Ads Manager will charge you when your ad is delivered to an audience that is most likely to click the provided link, which will then direct them to your website. You will not be charged when the link is clicked, but you will be charged each time the ad is shown to someone who has a proven history of following the links provided in advertisements. This is important because it prevents you from being charged if the same person clicks on your link repeatedly, which can happen by mistake or as a result of a malicious intent to abuse and misuse your ad campaign.

At this stage, you will also choose where you would like your ad to be placed on the Facebook platform. Ads may be displayed in the desktop News Feed, the mobile News Feed, or in the column to the right (outside of the News Feed). Displaying your ad in the column to the right could be beneficial, as those ads are typically stationary and do not scroll away as the user scrolls up and down through their News Feed. Advertising in that right-hand column can generate more attention, or more consistent attention, from Facebook users.

On the other hand - displaying your ad here may not provide greater attention, as many Facebook users rarely let their eyes divert away from their actual News Feed. There is no guarantee, so you may want to try a different ad campaign in each location, just to see what will work best for your ad sets and your business.

When choosing your ad location, take your demographics and target audience into serious consideration.

For example - should an ad be shown in the desktop News Feed or the mobile News Feed if the target audience is between 18 and 24 years of age? It should probably appear in the mobile News Feed, as this age group is much more likely to access Facebook on their mobile phones than on an actual computer.

Or - should an ad be shown in the desktop News Feed or the mobile News Feed if the target audience is between 65 and 80 years of age? It should probably appear in the desktop News Feed, as this age group probably does not access Facebook on their mobile phones, and if they do, they may find it difficult to read or interact with your ad set on such a small screen.

Tip: Choose multiple placement options to give your ads the best chance of engagement.

Tip: If you believe that one ad set is performing better than another, change just one of the ad settings, like: bidding, budget, placement, or targeting. Keep all other settings the same. This will reveal which setting is having the most impact, allowing you to learn more about the demographics connected to your business brand, what works, and what does not work.

Step four

The fourth step is to create a variety of ads and see which of those ads work best for your goals. You can use a combination of text, links, images, and video, and you can use up to fifty different ads in any given ad set. If one ad, in particular, is performing poorly, you can easily turn that ad off without altering or stopping the rest of your ad campaign, and without upsetting your budget. Best of all - Facebook Ads Manager never charges you for stopping or altering your ad campaign.

Keep in mind that your ads need to be eye-catching. Otherwise, audience members will scroll right past them without ever looking at what you have to present.

• Video Ads: keep the video short and make sure any audio attached to the video is neither too loud nor too quiet. Studies show that most people will click away from any ad video that lasts longer than twenty seconds.

• Image Ads: keep the images small enough to display nicely on a cell phone screen, and try to include some text on or around the image. Without the text, many audience members may be unsure of what it is you are advertising or what your objective is.

Another important thing to keep in mind when designing your ads is copyright laws. Be extremely careful with the images and videos that you use. Take advantage of websites like Shutterstock.com, whether you can safely purchase images or videos that are relevant to your product, brand, or company. Or, better yet, take the photos or videos yourself!

If your ad includes an image or video that you found via a quick Google search, and you did not obtain the appropriate copyright release, the owner of that image or video could allege theft, could send a "Cease & Desist" letter that would require you to stop using the image or video, and could even sue you and collect some of the profits that you saw as a result of the ad campaign their image or video was used in. Copyright laws are surprisingly strict, and if there is a copyright dispute, it can be a very stressful and costly situation.

Similar to copyright laws are "intellectual property laws," which are what protect writers from plagiarism. Be careful with what you write in your ad copy. You will want to make sure the text is original. You can do this by using various plagiarism checkers that are free to use online, like www.edubirdie.com.

Step five

Once your ad set has been published, it is very important to pay attention to ad performance. Some ads may perform better than others, and you will need to find out why one ad performs better than others; that way, you can adjust your ad set (and future ad sets) accordingly.

Facebook Ads Manager allows you to turn a particular ad off if you need to. You can also cancel your ad campaign altogether. In addition, if the parameters you set for your campaign are not generating any results, Facebook Ads Manager may waive the expense of the campaign, or reimburse you if they have already collected payment.

Keep in mind that Facebook Ads Manager only bills you once a month, and only bills you for what has been spent on your ad campaign. Therefore - if you set a lifetime budget of $500 for your ad campaign, but only $25 of that $500 is spent in the month of January, then Facebook Ads Manager will only collect the $25 spent in January. This type of pay-as-you-go billing is incredibly useful for small businesses and those with small advertising budgets. Billing can be set up on an auto-pay schedule, using any major card. The auto-pay schedule can be customized so that you can even choose the day of the month that your payment is automatically withdrawn from your bank account or charged to your selected credit card.

Tip: It is better to turn off an ad or ad set as opposed to completely deleting them. Deleting an ad or ad set is irreversible. Turning an ad or ad set off is like hitting that pause button. This way, you can turn them back on later, if necessary, and after you have adjusted whatever parameter was preventing your ad from performing well. You can also turn the ad set off if you suddenly find that you need to make an emergency change to your advertising budget.

What Will It Cost? – Effective Budgeting for Your Facebook Campaign

I.   Budget

Creating and maintaining a budget with Facebook Ads Manager is easy. You can tailor every aspect of the ad campaign to fit within your budget, and the Ads Manager will quickly let you know if your budget is too small for your goals.

Facebook Ads Manager refers to your budget as an "Auction." The Auction determines which ads are shown to which audiences, based on the demographics you choose. The ad is always shown to the audience that is most likely to be interested, and once the price (or bid) is set, Facebook Ads Manager will never show your ad in a way that might exceed your bid, or what you are willing to spend on the campaign in question.

During the ad creation process, you will set specific parameters, including:

• Budget: This is the total amount you are willing to spend over the course of the campaign - whether the campaign is scheduled to last one day, one month, or longer. You can edit your budget at any time, but you will be asked to set a maximum amount that Facebook Ads Manager will never exceed without your express permission.

• Audience: This tool allows you to choose who sees your ad campaign. Your audience can be tailored depending on age, gender, or location.

• Creative: This tool allows you to choose how your ad appears - whether you use text, images, or videos to capture the attention of your target audience.

Facebook Ads Manager Also Provides Two Specialty Buying Options, Reach & Frequency, and Target Rating Points.

• Reach & Frequency: This specialty buying option is ideal if your campaign needs to target more than 200,000 people. It provides controlled ad delivery at a locked price. For more information, visit the Facebook Business page at: https://www.Facebook.com/business/learn/facebook-reach-and-frequency-buying

• Target Rating Points: This specialty buying option allows you to purchase video ads on Facebook, much like you would if you were purchasing television ads on a national network. For more information, visit the Facebook Business FAQ page at https://www.facebook.com/business/help/518993728299293

Facebook ad campaigns can cost you as little as $5.00 a week, or as much as $50,000 a week. This aspect is highly customizable. Once a budget is set, Facebook Ad Manager will automatically calculate the "audience reach," based on your budget and the length of time you have chosen to run the campaign. If you want your ad to reach a wider audience, you can either increase your budget or reduce the length of your ad campaign.

The Ads Manager will also calculate the cost per result for you. If you, or your client, want to set a budget based on the cost per result (instead of a budget based on the campaign as a whole), this calculation is the one you will need to look at most closely.

In addition, Facebook Ads Manager allows you to tailor your budget even further in the following ways:

• Campaign Spending Limit: This parameter allows you to set the maximum amount you are willing to spend on the advertising campaign in question. This is your overall budget for a SINGLE ad.

• Account Spending Limit: This parameter allows you to set a maximum amount you are willing to spend on ALL of your campaigns, not just one particular ad.

Given the specific requirements of your advertising campaign, like the budget, bid, or targeted audience, the Ads Manager will give you an estimate of how many people your advertisement will reach before you actually publish the ad. This is especially useful if you or your client are unsure about your budget or audience.

Once your ad campaign has been published, you will receive performance updates throughout the campaign. These results are available on the "Insights" tab in the Ads Manager. It is very important to take these updates into consideration throughout the campaign, as adjustments to the campaign parameters may be necessary to hit your performance goals - like increasing your budget or reducing or expanding your audience.

If, for some reason, your ad campaign is completely unsuccessful, and Facebook Ads Manager is unable to obtain the results that were quoted to you when the ad was published - whether the issue is related to your budget or your ad strategy - Facebook Ads Manager will stop delivering the ad, and you will not be charged if you did not receive results. This "guarantee" is especially important for first-time advertisers and small business owners that have a tight advertising budget.

Delivering Ad Campaigns

Facebook Ads Manager goes to great lengths to ensure that your ad campaign is only seen by an audience interested in what you are advertising. This prevents audience members from issuing complaints about advertisements that are not relevant to them, and it prevents you from spending your advertising budget in a manner that is not beneficial to your business or brand.

The goal of the Facebook Ads Manager is to make sure that the right ad is seen by the right audience at the right time. This is different from traditional advertising, which is focused more on the "value" of an ad. Traditionally, several ad agencies will create a campaign based on your proposal, and would then submit bids in an effort to obtain the contract. Those campaigns are then evaluated from a monetary standpoint; typically, the cheapest campaign would be chosen.

With Facebook Ads Manager, you can obtain the results you want on almost any budget - as you are in complete control of the parameters you set for your campaign. Even if someone else sets a higher ad budget, your ad may still reach more audience members or have better overall performance. It is entirely up to you, and with Facebook Ads Manager, you have every tool you need to guarantee success in your ad campaign.

Ad Auctions

A Facebook Ad Auction determines which advertisements are shown to which customers or users, based on the information provided during the ad creation process and the structuring of the ad campaign. The Auction ensures that your ad is shown to customers or users who are "most likely" to be interested in your business, product, or brand - and it makes sure that your ad is never shown to those customers at a higher price than was agreed upon in your budget.

Facebook Ad Auctions use the following parameters to determine which ad is seen by which user:

• Budget: At this point, you will have already set a budget for your ad campaign - both your daily budget and your "ad lifetime" budget.
• Audience: At this point, you will have chosen your audience by age, gender, location, and more.
• Creative: This refers to your ad design - whether it is an image, a video, text only, a slideshow, et cetera.
In addition to those parameters, Facebook Ad Auctions also offer two unique "ad buying options."
• Reach & Frequency: This option is ideal if you want your ad to reach more than 200,000 people. It gives you a predictable ad cycle on a set budget.
• Target Rating Points: For those accustomed to purchasing television ads, this is very similar. You can use this option if you are interested in purchasing video ads.

Facebook Ad Auctions always run within the budget you set when you designed your ad campaign. You can spend as little as $5 per week or as much $50,000 per week. The cost of your campaign is broken down into these categories:
• Campaign Spending Limit: this is the maximum amount you are willing to spend on the entire ad campaign.

- Account Spending Limit: this is the maximum amount you are willing to spend on every ad campaign on your account.

Using these two limits, and the parameters provided when you designed your ad campaign, Facebook Ads Manager, will then provide you with an estimate of how many people or customers they expect your ad to reach - all before you actually publish your ad! This will allow you to think, yet again, about your ad budget and whether or not you need to increase it. Remember - Facebook Ads Manager will never exceed the budget you set. Facebook Ad Auctions also seek to make sure that you always achieve the results you expect to achieve while making sure that the customers never see ads that are not relevant to them. This keeps both parties happy and provides a positive experience for all involved.

When a Facebook Ad Auction takes place, Facebook uses the information provided in a customer's profile to match them with several different ads. The ad that is ultimately displayed for that customer is the ad that will cost the least amount to display. This guarantees that the ad marketplace is fair and unbiased and that advertising accounts never receive preference or special treatment. The decision is based entirely on the budget of the ad campaign and whether or not the ad is suitable for the customer in question.

Each time your ad is displayed, Facebook Ads Manager will then use part of your previously determined budget to pay for that ad. Facebook Ads Manager will always use the smallest amount of your budget funds possible. This means you will frequently be charged less than you anticipated, and you will rarely need to increase your budget to achieve your original goals. You should only ever need to increase your budget if you have determined that your ad campaign is more successful than expected - and therefore, you decide to run the campaign for a longer period of time than originally planned.

Final Thoughts

- Respect copyright laws! Make sure your ad content is either completely original, or that you have obtained the necessary copyright releases for the images, videos, or other content you may be using.
- Utilize the reports available within the Facebook Ads Manager! With these reports, you can learn exactly how to create and manage a successful and profitable ad campaign, time, and time again.
- Choose your audience carefully! A narrow audience may be ideal for strictly targeted ad campaigns, but a broad audience may be better if you are looking to increase overall profits or website traffic.
- Your budget is not set in stone! Facebook Ads Manager makes it incredibly easy to tailor your budget to your needs, without ever going

over-budget. You can add money at any time, and Facebook will only ever bill you on a month-to-month basis - never charging for what has not been used in the campaign.

Finally, we would greatly appreciate your feedback in the form of an Amazon review, especially if you found this guide to be informative and helpful.

CHAPTER 5
Airbnb

Airbnb is an online marketplace that provides the opportunity to rent the property or room to tourists or visitors. Airbnb has set a 3 percent commission on every deal from the hosts and 6-12 percent from the tourists. It is a third party platform launched in San Francisco in August 2008. Airbnb offers its customers to search the property according to their needs through different criteria. For example, if someone is looking for a room only or a full home, then he/she can filter it through the property type. Moreover, if you want a garden or swimming pool in the rental space, Airbnb also helps you find them through its filters. Every property has its description as well as pictures attached to it. Currently, it is operating in over 191 countries and lists 1.5 million properties or rooms.

Why Is It Popular?

Well, it has a number of factors for receiving appreciation from the public all around the globe. The most significant and top of the list reason behind the popularity is the financial one. Tourists are able to find good accommodations at comfortable rates without any problem. The prices are comparatively at a low rate from the hotels at any location in the world. Similarly, the platform also has a great incentive for the hosts. They can use their room at any point in time. This means, if kids are at summer camp, then their parents can utilize the free space on Airbnb for a few days. Later, they can remove the room from listing when kids are back.

Steps for Converting a Rental to Airbnb

Listing your property is simple on Airbnb but requires some steps to complete. However, you would require to do some research in order to find what are the trending rates for the type of property you own.

1.1. Adding the Property/Room
Airbnb provides the categories to list your property according to the categories. You have to provide details regarding the number of rooms, kitchen, bathroom, and other features of the property. In the case of a room, you will fill out the details related to furniture, area, and electronic items, etc.

1.2. Setting the Price

This will require you to do a comparative analysis with the other people offering the rentals at your location. Simply, filter out your city and the matching category of property you are looking to rent out to tourists. After that, you can see the listings on a map with the price offered. You have the choice to offer a 75 percent price to attract customers. In any case, do not over-price your space.

1.3. Description of the Property/Room
Short term rental customers have a different mentality as compared to that of long term rentals. They take rented rooms or property not only as living space, but they consider it to be an experience. Therefore, you must provide the details related to the features of the property. Do not provide it as a list of times instead write a detail related to what experience they will have with the features available. Moreover, the title should have the required advantage of the property, for example, " Quite an Apartment, Perfect for romantic walks late at night at the beach."

1.4. Images and Photos
It has critical importance in the marketing of your property/room. Therefore, the images must be in high definition format with a clear view of features. Images bring in bookings more than anything on your Airbnb portfolio. Therefore, try to insert at least 20 images with a focus on describing each and every feature through them. Apart from this, make sure that your property and room comprises everything that your display image is showing to the tourists. Otherwise, there will be negative feedback on your listing at Airbnb. Besides this, keep editing the image list with anything you have updated with the room.

How to Maximize Profits?

Well, this ain't the goal of every business in the market? Certainly, Yes. Every business owner looks to increase the quality of its service and promotion to attract larger customers in order to generate more income. Correspondingly, Airbnb requires some effective measures to get a boost towards your passive income earnings. Here, we will provide you top ideas to achieve this goal at Airbnb.

2.1. Maximum Sleeping Arrangements
The formula is simple at Airbnb, the more you can host, the more revenue you can gain. For master bedrooms, you can advertise it as a single bed. However, in other rooms, it is ideal to place two double beds for maximum sleeping options. For example, your room can have a double bunk bed or sofa-cum-bed for this purpose.

2.2. Earn 5-Star Ratings

Most of the clients or tourists look for ratings when choosing between similar options for rent at Airbnb. Therefore, try to build the trust factor by getting 5-star reviews from the guests after the departure. This can be attained by providing the best possible customer service and features that you advertise at Airbnb.

Airbnb SEO

Search Engine Optimization concepts can be utilized at the Airbnb website. You can do it by following actions.

1. Make sure you have set an instant book option. This means tourists can book property without consulting hosts. It is observed by experts that Airbnb shows properties higher with instant book options.
2. Make minimum stay options for one night.
3. Response as a host should be quick to stay higher on the search results.
4. Earn five-star rankings from the tourists or customers. Moreover, share your 5-star rankings on social media.

Airbnb has been one of the most promising online platforms in recent years. Its popularity is growing with time all around the world. It can be a great source of passive income for people having free space for accommodation. However, it requires a little effort to welcome the customers and make sure everything is working fine regarding the space offered at Airbnb. Give it a try if you have all the features available to set up a platform for passive income at your home.

CHAPTER 6
Instagram

Instagram was launched in 2010 by its owners and later on acquired by Mark Zuckerberg (Facebook Owner) in 2012. Instagram took social media users by storm through its features. People all around the world were attracted to the unique style of interactive content creation and sharing options by the app. It allows you to share and take rendered images through its own software. The work of the designers and developers deserves most appreciation behind the overall features of the app.

Apart from its main feature of social interaction today, Instagram has become a strong force in the field of marketing. Currently, the total number of users of Instagram are in millions all across the globe. Hence, it's not a surprise for anyone that many international and local brands are utilizing this platform to advertise their services and products. Similarly, you also have the chance to earn money through it if you are willing to put some extra effort at the start. The passive income earned through Instagram only requires to use your mobile while sitting at home. The world of Instagram contains a number of opportunities for you to earn passive income. Here, we are suggesting a few below, read them carefully to implement.

Engagement Boosting

This method involves the influencing of followers by the account handlers. Basically, Instagram users with large followers help the small account owners by promoting them with their community. In other words, small account handlers will pay you money to engage your account in their posts. Moreover, brands are also looking for local Instagram handlers with a large fan base to promote their products. For this, you just have to make sure that you have a strong following on Instagram. However, if you don't have then, please read our tips below to help you find the mark.

- Make use of hashtags and keywords in your Instagram bio and details page. The hashtags and keywords should be used as compulsory in the posts.
- The consistency in posting is required in the early days. The more content you generate, the more it will reach the audience.
- To interact with your followers and other accounts to provide a view of your personality in order to attract users.

Affiliate Marketing

Many of the Instagram users are earning passive income by simply promoting the brand or product through images and videos. You just have to post an image with the product and refer it to the affiliate link to get paid from the owners. It is a common method of earning passive income in the fashion industry. Moreover, people having travel pages can also utilize platforms to attract brands. The main concept behind this idea is that the product you are promoting is part of your lifestyle.

Digital Real Estate

Most of the Instagram users won't be familiar with the method to earn money through Instagram. However, you will surely have the idea of flipping the home. Digital real estate works quite the same way. Influencers with large following options to purchase the accounts to make them grow using their influence on the community. Moving on, when the account has achieved the desired level of following and appreciation, then it is sold at a profitable margin. It requires no such physical effort but using the same tricks, which helped you in growing the personal account. Although, it is a time-consuming experience and the help of engagement boosting from the self-account helps you complete the task as soon as possible. This method of generating passive income is attracting lots of entrepreneurs to this platform.

Sell Photos

Remember, in our introductory chapters, we discuss the term passion working is crucial for generating passive income. If you have a passion for photography, then you can also utilize it for commercial purposes. You just have to place a watermark on your awesome shots, which contain the contact details for purchasing the pictures. Your Instagram followers and big agencies will be ready to buy your pictures according to their choice. This method is exciting for you as it involves your passion, which won't let you get bored out of it at any point in time.

The above-discussed methods will require you some initial hard work and consistency. However, all of them will turn out to be beneficial for earning passive income with little effort later on.

Top Marketplaces for earning money on Instagram

Instead of putting effort into outreaching, you have the chance to explore already present opportunities. Take a look at them one by one.

Tribe

It is a well-developed Android and iOS app which helps the agents, talent, and influencers get connected to the brands and one another. As a user, you can browse different brands available and tag them in the posts to earn money.

Influicity

Primarily working as a platform for influencers to bring in money-making opportunities through working with brands. As an influencer, you have the chance to get content creation jobs by setting up your profile. You have to complete a detailed form describing you and the followers you have.

Hyprbrands

According to their claim, they have the largest database of influencers all over the world. They utilize social analytics tools for their operations. Brands have the luxury to analyze all the posts from the influencers in terms of demographics, views, and sales.

These were some of the top marketplaces for Instagram users with large followers for earning passive income. Moreover, you can also use more platforms such as Hyper tab, Fame bit, and Revfluence.

CHAPTER 7
Rental Properties

As previously discussed in section Real Estate, it is one of the oldest methods to earn passive income through rental properties. The dream of relaxing at home with the consistent cash flow gets really better than any other field in rental properties. It only requires an initial investment in acquiring the rental property. Due to this reason, experts recommend it to be the best method to earn passive income all over the world.

Rental Income

What makes it feel better than receiving the check at the start of each month without any effort? This is purely the best reason why rental properties business is the most popular option for earning passive income. However, if you are looking for positive cash flow, then it is important to invest in the property that has a positive value. The market is full of properties having positive and negative geared values. It is certain that investment is positively geared value property yields positive cash flow. Therefore, in order to make sure you invest in the right one, you should make yourself familiar with the real estate analytics tool available online. It provides you a complete analysis of the cap rate, cash on return, and rental income.

No Involvement

As a property owner, you have the opportunity of avoiding any kind of physical involvement during the process. In the market, there are many investment firms operating that take care of the tasks on behalf of property owners. Professional property management completes the daily operations related to the property, which include rent collection, record management, and handling deals of the tenants. Moreover, it might be surprising for you that these companies also take care of legal matters. The other side of the story is that these companies will charge you for providing these services. Hence, when planning your cash flow from the property, it is advised to include professional property management fees.

Part-Time Investment

Rental properties are considered to be ideal for people who want to do some part-time business. This means that in the rental properties field or business, you can comfortably focus on a 9-5 job. The passive income will be consistently coming without dealing it in during the regular job. Nevertheless, getting yourself completely out of the process can result in a negative way. You should take knowledge from the professional property management company at regular intervals. Make sure you are up to date regarding any kind of financial activity related to your property.

These advantages are certainly attractive to anyone who is looking to make an investment in a business. However, before making any investment, take some guidelines from the experts related to buying any property for commercial purposes.

Myths Related to Rental Business

If you bring in discussion related to property investment in any gathering, then be ready for different opinions. You may hear from some as it is great to invest in rental properties, while others may present you some myths to prove it is a bad decision to invest. These myths make people confused related to renting business. They often have strong arguments with them, but in reality, the case is altogether different. In this section, you will get to read some of the most popular myths towards rental business and our clarification related to them.

2.1. Need to be Rich

Many people have the misconception that it requires rich status to enter in the property business. Nonetheless, in reality, you have plenty of options to launch a property portfolio without spending much money. The most popular option for this situation is to get into partnership with investors having enough financial resources. In the real estate world, "If you have analyzed the whole project and found it to be profitable, then capital is never out of reach to start it." Just be brave and take the bold decision to get into the rental business if you wish to.

2.2. Debt is Bad

Many children are raised with the mindset that borrowing is a bad strategy for anything. Therefore, if someone gives you an idea about debt, then it may seem counterintuitive to your mind. Loans and debts are available from banking channels to property and real estate businessmen. The interest rate of the bank loan can be easily paid back if you make good investment in property. The rental income pays you enough to submit installments of a loan, excluding monthly profits.

2.3. Bad Credit Scores puts Hurdles in Investing

It is a common perception that bad credit scores make it impossible to get investment for the rental business. It can be true about the banking channels; however, they are not the only channel to get investment.

When the plan is well projected and organized, then investors can find capital from a number of alternative channels.

2.4. Property Investment is Long-Term

The traditional mindset related to the rental business is that it takes a lot of time to be profitable. Nonetheless, if your financial calculations are right, then it can leave you with some profit from day one. You just have to make sure that the passive income you earn from a rental property is enough to repay loan installments. It may seem hard, but it is not impossible if you plan to investigate purchases with different channels.

The above arguments show that a certain viewpoint related to the rental and property business are not correct. Therefore, if you are planning on a real estate business, then make sure you have done the proper research work. Overall, rental properties can earn you passive income if you can make up the capital in the early days. The passive income earned through rental income can be consistent enough to get you out of any kind of financial trouble.

CHAPTER 8
Virtual Assistant

Virtual assistant refers to the professional who is self-employed and looks to provide professional assistance to learners on various topics. The virtual assistants usually operate from a remote location to their clients. These virtual assistants are independent contractors, which means clients are not responsible for employee taxes. Unless the fees of a virtual assistant include these taxes from clients. The main resource used for communication of information by the virtual assistants is the internet, conference calls, or email. However, with time these options are increasing in the form of Skype, WhatsApp, or even Facebook. The virtual assistants mostly come up from the business field with years of experience in their specific field.

Virtual Assistants have found their way in the mainstream business, such as in the form of Voice Over Internet Protocol (VOIP). On the other hand, companies also operate in the form of virtual assistants that provide products and services to clients from a remote location. The business of these companies is growing with time, and their revenue is ever increasing. Some of the most popular virtual assistant companies are:

- Boldly
- Livelink Resource
- VOIP Terminator

The virtual assistant business can be a great source for earning passive income by a skilled person. As a service business owner, you have a number of opportunities in front of you related to the virtual assistant field. The key to earning passive income, in this case, is to set up an automated system so that you make almost no effort. It is obviously true that your workload cuts down with an efficient self-sustaining system in your hand. However, to implement such a system, you need to have some good ideas in your mind. Here, we will suggest you some of the self-sustaining automated systems for passive income below. Read them carefully to understand and implement it.

Sell Evergreen Products

When you are selling a product, make sure that it has usage by the clients all over the year. For instance, when you are training people related to the Christmas celebration, then it may be popular at the end of the year only. Evergreen products or services means they are in constant demand of the public. The options for this type of products is to write or sell an e-book or conduct online webinars related to technical education or information technology.

Sales Funnel

Every business has the requirement of a well-functioning sales funnel on their website these days. However, in the case of a passive income stream, sales funnel is critically important for a successful venture. The sales funnel should be comprehensive enough to lead your clients towards your sales without letting you do any task. In order to prepare an effective sales to funnel, you should follow the below recommendations;

- Sales Landing Page
- Campaign covering all social media apps and websites
- Email marketing
- Blogs advertising your services

Integrating E-commerce

The dream of passive income can also be turned into reality through e-commerce. A virtual assistant can utilize online shopping carts for integrating eCommerce stores on its website. This will satisfy the need of your clients to go through a pleasant shopping experience from your website with the availability of multiple options.

The automation system can earn you passive income on a long term basis. However, setting up an automation system cannot be termed as passive since it requires a lot of effort at the start by the entrepreneur.

Ideas for Passive Income Through Virtual Assistant

1. Tutorial Channel

Create youtube videos on different education subjects or tutorials for learning any tool, language, or any other skill. This way, people can search and watch your videos with keeping learning objectives in mind. If you manage to get good enough views and subscribers on your tutorials, then there will be a lot of passive income coming through ads.

2. Hosting Reseller

Clients operating businesses require websites at must these days in the era of technology. Therefore, it is obvious that they would need web hosting for this purpose. You will be surprised to know that many companies are offering reselling programs online. Therefore, you just have to submit a fee to become a reseller. After that, start selling web hosting to the clients with your own brand name.

3. E-books
People are looking for books on various topics online. You just need to research a good idea for writing up a book and then sell it on the online platform such a Kindle Publishing.

4. Sponsorships
This is the most common method to earn passive income since the advent of the internet era. If you are running a blog or a video channel, then earning money through sponsorships is a very simple process. You just have to place a link to a client website or product in the details or comments section to receive cash flow from them.

5. Podcast
It can be explained as an episodic series of audios and videos on any topic which the user has to download for listening. You can promote a business through the podcast, and in return, they can pay you for this. It works on the business model of affiliate marketing. Moreover, you can use a podcast for generating passive income by selling these audios and videos to the user.

6. Plugin
Blogging has been one of the most popular modern professions in the world. However, to make it easier, there are a number of plugins available online. You can also create a plugin or hire someone to do it. After that, just do strong marketing and earn money through online selling of the plugin to the bloggers.

7. Sign Up Offer
After making some video, audio, or written tutorial, make sure that watching or downloading them requires a signup process. In this way, you can promote a product of your own or do some affiliate marketing for any other company.

Three Drivers of Virtual Assistant Business

The virtual Assistant business has three drivers that urge people to make use of the services or products offered by it.

1. **Income**
    Make your audience realize through marketing and your stuff that the service you offer is helpful for them in order to earn some income. For example, online tutor courses can be promoted as critical to growing skills for getting money-making opportunities.

2. **Impact**
    What is the overall effect of your assistance to the business and life of the clients? If you manage to create an impact, then your clients would be ready to pay you anything for assistance.

3. **Influence**
Your assistance must be influential to help grow the business of the client. In the case of a video tutorial, make your students feel that this training is crucial for their future.

Tips for Running Your Virtual Assistance Business

In previous sections, you have read some useful ideas to generate passive income through virtual assistants. Now, we will guide you on how to set up a virtual assistant business to earn passive or active income.

1. **Read, Research and Network**
When you are working as a virtual assistant, it may seem like you are working alone, and you have to do everything on your own. However, you have the option of consulting at online forums, websites, and books. Research can help you narrow down the services you are offering to the clients. Moreover, if you are able to make a network with other virtual assistants, then you also have the choice of outsourcing your work.

2. **Expand Skills**
Virtual assistants have to complete multiple tasks rather than just performing job-specific duties. As a virtual assistant, you have to take care of all the operations that are critical for running the business. You must be experienced enough to handle business administration activities. Apart from this, clients expect high-quality skills from virtual assistants all over the world. Therefore, make sure that your skills are well-polished in the office environment before opting for assisting virtually.

3. **Clear Communication**

Virtual assistants have to face severe difficulties in case their communications with the clients are not clear. The reason behind this situation is that there are no daily interactions, such as in-office work. Usually, tasks performed by the virtual assistants have high importance for the business of clients. Therefore, to keep them satisfied, proper flow and communication of information must be on the top of your priority list as a virtual assistant.

4. Adapt with Clients

As a virtual assistant, clients are the most important factor in your business. Hence, you should be able to deliver the exact work that the client is demanding from you. You should work as a restaurant manager who is looking to provide anything customer demands from the menu.

Pros of Virtual Assistant Business

There are a number of advantages and benefits a virtual assistant business provides to you. This is why its demand is growing day by day.

- It can be started free without any financial investment. You have no requirements to purchase heavy types of equipment or office.
- It is flexible to work as a virtual assistant. Moreover, passive income options like podcasts, videos, or books can be almost effortless after the initial work.
- Working as an independent professional is almost the dream of every job holder. This can be done with a virtual assistant business.
- Just as the name suggests, it is location independent. This means that if you are traveling somewhere, then you can still work remotely.
- There is no degree requirement for doing a job as a virtual assistant. All you need is the required skill set for performing the job.

Cons of Virtual Assistant Business

- Getting your first client can prove to be a tough task in the virtual assistant business. However, you can get going well after the initial hard work.
- As you are working as an independent contractor, therefore, you don't have any privileges in the form of employee benefits.
- We have mentioned this in the introduction paragraph of this section that most of the time, the virtual assistant has to pay its taxes on their own.

- As a lonely worker, it may impact you mentally or psychologically. You may find it to be boring at times and feel dissatisfied with the environment.

To conclude, a virtual assistant business is a great source of passive income for professionals around the globe. However, everyone should complete the prerequisites in order to achieve success in this field.

CHAPTER 9
Network Marketing

Network marketing also referred to as multilevel or pyramid marketing, is a business model that relies on person to person sales. The sales process is operated by independent representatives who are performing their tasks at home. The work-force is non-salaried and depends upon the income earned on the basis of selling the products or services. The commission system works on the pyramid basis, which will be described in detail to you later on.

How Does it Work?

Companies with a network marketing business opt to hire different tiers of salespersons. Companies also encourage the hired salespersons to recruit people under themselves to create more networks of salespersons. The salesperson who creates the tier earns dual income by the commission earned by making itself and that of the tier created by him/her. With some time, a downline tier can create another tier, which will add more income to the person at the top. Therefore, the earnings in this business model depend on recruitment and sales. Whoever gets the chance to enter first and makes their way top the top tier earns the most. The tier aspect is further divided into different categories to explain to you for understanding.

1.1. Single Tier Network Marketing
It is the beginning of your work in network marketing. You have to get registered with the affiliate program without any fixed salary. The source of income, as discussed earlier, relies on commission earned through selling their products and services. In some programs, you get paid for diverting the traffic to the website or app of the client.

1.2. Two Tier Networking
This system provides you the earnings based on the sales you made for the business company and the people who are hired by you to work for you. It is a two-tier work in which the top tier employee hires subordinates or creates downline salespersons by itself to sell products of the company.

1.3. Multi-Tier Networking
These programs expand the network further from two-tier to multi-tier business models. In this case, the workers hired by you can recruit more people under themselves to sell more products and services.

Passive Income Through Network Marketing

We hope you have learned enough to understand how actually network marketing works. Now, let's come to our basic topic to generate ideas for passive income. The question here is how to use the network marketing field to build up a consistent stream for passive income. The network marketing fields you to set up a system where you can earn money without directly selling the items. Passive income can come up within the network marketing operations in a number of ways.

As discussed in detail earlier, network marketing has a system of downline. The advantage of this system is that you can earn money by getting a percentage of the commission earned by the downline salesperson or workers hired by you. Therefore, if you manage to hire a large downline or even a couple of good sellers, then we assure you that you have cleared the way for handsome passive income coming towards you again and again. Just imagine if you have 4 or 5 downline levels of salespersons working under you and calculate the percentage of the commission from their sales. The passive income earned from such a downline won't require you to do any kind of effort to product or services yourself.

In modern days, many businesses operate online to sell their stuff. This makes passive income more reachable for you in the network marketing field. It ain't require a physical system to make sales and make a record of it. For this, the website does all the work for you, and automated systems can take care of the sales record and calculate all the percentage of commission from the downline. As a top tier salesperson, you just have to make sure that the downline is maintaining the record in the right way. Therefore, just when your website is operational, sales of products will start to happen, and you can earn money even when you are out of town or on vacation. This enables you to try some new marketing strategies for earning money as the regular passive income is coming into your account from the downline.

Passive income is what people around the world strive for. In network marketing, it is a common procedure for doing business. If you are planning to give it a try, then please go ahead because it feels amazing to have such an income source in which you are not working physically at all.

Top Opportunities for Passive Income in Network Marketing

Network marketing or multilevel marketing is a business whose popularity has grown amazingly in recent years. Entrepreneurs are eager to take a step in this field to earn passive income from multiple sources. Moreover, this process is also providing great advantages for companies to sell their products through workers from remote locations. These companies are offering opportunities to the common public to earn income through network marketing. Take a look at the top opportunities available in the market with whom you can take benefit from.

3.1. Do Terra
The trend of using natural stuff has contributed to the usage of essential oils among the public. The essential oils are utilized in different fields, such as in beauty products, roller blinds, and cleaning items. Do Terra is one of the leading brands selling essential oils. It is using the business model of network marketing and has almost over 3 million distributors operating. The numbers are ever-increasing, which makes it a great opportunity for you to start your network marketing strategy to earn passive income. You can make use of the social media marketing team to help buyers purchase the products through your referral code. This will result in income coming to you while you are staying at home.

3.2. Young Living
This is another network marketing company selling essential oils, which gives an assessment of how popular essential oils are these days. It started its operations in 1993 and has helped essential oils to become a household name. The opportunities it provides for passive income is through its excellent commission rates, tiered packages, and membership benefits. However, it helps you earn income in the same way as Do Terra by identifying the referral code sent by you.

3.3. Avon
It has a global market reach and mainly produces products related to beauty and hygiene for men and women. Apart from this, the company is also looking to mark its impact on the clothing and shoe industry. It also follows a network marketing strategy by hiring people on a commission basis all over the world to sell their products. Due to their popularity in the female circle, their revenue is increasing with time, which indicates a good income for you in the future.

3.4. Forever Living
It is a US-based company that is manufacturing health, aloe vera, and skincare products. According to the estimates, this company is maintaining the largest channel of manufacturing and distribution of products. However, the good thing is its distribution network follows the same method as the above companies. This provides you the opportunity to hire downline workers to sell products with your referral code to

enable you to earn passive income while you are just staying at home. Nonetheless, for starting the distribution of products, you have to submit a registration fee worth 90 to 250 US Dollars.

3.5. Tupperware
You must have heard Tupperware's name due to its products related to home-based accessories. It has a great market around the world with the most sales as compared to the other household products manufacturing companies. Hence, with such huge sales, it is ideal for you to start with this company to grow your network marketing structure in order to generate passive income consistently.

In the end, there are a number of opportunities available for you related to network marketing. It is becoming one of the top options to have a side income source for professionals. All you need is to build up a downline with professional people who will be critical for you to find the desired mark in this field. However, a positive attitude regarding the job is required in the early stages of a career in this field to build up a long term passive income stream for yourself. We hope that our recommendations regarding the companies and explanation of the whole process will help you enter the field with enough knowledge to make wise choices and decisions.

CHAPTER 10
Vending Machine

If you are searching for a business that doesn't need specific skills to operate and can be done part-time with the help of your family and friends, then we are suggesting one for you here. Vending Machine, a modern-day business opportunity that has been making a gross of 7 Billion Dollars in the USA every year. You must have used a vending machine once in your life in a mall, hospital, or any other place. Usually, it contains food and drinking materials that come out after you put a coin, code, or cash in it. However, most of these operate on a cash basis, while some of them are also compatible with the credit cards. They are found to be placed in almost all of the big cities in every country. In recent times, vending machines are turning into specialized ones which contain only specific products of a company.

The first modern-day vending machine was introduced in the 1880s in London. From that point on, there is a continuous introduction of new features and facilities related to the vending machines. Currently, these vending machines are working in different categories, such as snacks, bill changers, food, and frozen items. It requires you to input credit card details, cash, or code to purchase the product. It mainly provides you the items in two ways.

- The machine releases the product, and it falls at the bottom of the machine as soon as payment is made by the person.
- The door of the machine is unlocked to pick up the items.

Passive Income By Vending Machine Business

Many people invest in prominent businesses such as real estate to set up a passive income stream for themselves. However, these businesses might require certain skills and knowledge to achieve success. As a job holder, you would be looking for a business that does not require heavy effort and still gets you the consistent cash flow. In this scenario, the vending machine business is the best possible choice for you to earn passive income. It may sound weird to you as it is not the commonly discussed business idea. Nonetheless, if you do it properly with the set plan, then be ready to receive some consistent bucks in your bank account. The great thing about this business is that it can be managed easily and does not require any heavy upfront investment.

The concept of vending machines is a perfect example of a passive income business model. As an owner, you are selling the stuff through machines without any headache of handling the customers. They simply put in the money and take out the required product or item. This means that your business is running without any consistent effort. However, it is your responsibility to restock it when the items inside it are not available. The idea of vending machine business is simple and easy to maintain, but it needs proper planning and research work in the start to achieve the desired target. In the next section, you will read the tips to set up a smart vending machine business for earning passive income.

Tips for Profitable Vending Machine Business

Although, the simplicity of the vending machine business makes it a recommended choice to invest your money on it. It needs to be done with homework and market analysis to make it profitable for you. Take a look at the following tips, which are critical for your vending machine business.

Choose the Right Location

Well, location is the most important factor in the vending machine business. If you manage to find a suitable location for your snack vending machine, then the chances of attaining the profit will rise up comprehensively. For choosing the right location to place a vending machine, consider the following factors while doing the market research. Find out the locations where the traffic is usually high all the time. For example, shopping malls, event centers, and educational institutes.

- The location where there are no such food options available around it.
- Offices where the total strength of the organization is more than 50.
- Areas where the public has to wait routinely whenever they visit it. For instance, a hospital or a private clinic of a doctor.

Matching Products

In any business, the products you offer must be in line with the location and the mindset of people around it. For example, you cannot install a bill renting a vending machine at a hospital or airport. People do not expect to come there with the idea of paying the bills. Nonetheless, snacks, drinks, or soda are such items that need to be found at any location. Yet, you need to analyze the location environment and choose products according to that. For instance, candy vending machines should be installed where kids are expected in large numbers, such as in parks or playgrounds.

Machine Lineup

Take a decision wisely while choosing the lineup of products you are offering to the customers. The recommended plan is to diversify your line up in a way that two or more products you are offering complement each other. For example, it is ideal to place soda and snack items, which are a perfect combination together. Moreover, investing in your stocks increases the lineup. You must take this decision on the basis of data on which type of products are more on-demand.

Alternative Payment Options

When a customer is purchasing the product outside, it has different preferences regarding the payment methods. While some of the people still trust the cash in pockets, however, many customers rely on credit cards. It is the best strategy to allow any kind of payment method to increase sales. This way, your customer won't have to go outside in search of an ATM to withdraw cash for purchasing items out of your vending machine.

Adding Extra Services

It is a great option to add some complementary services in the list offerings by your vending machines. One of the successful business options is to introduce pantry services in the offices of different organizations. In this method, you stock the office kitchen along with the options of different food items which are free to be enjoyed by the workers. This is done by the companies in order to satisfy their workers and keep them healthy.

The above-recommended factors are very important to run a successful vending business for earning passive income for the long term. Just do the smart work by researching the market and the current trends in food to enjoy a consistent cash flow without any significant effort.

CHAPTER 11
Start A Podcast

We have discussed the creation of your skills in our virtual assistant business section. Here, we will discuss it in more detail to make you understand how it can be used for earning passive income. The podcast is usually an episodic series containing audio and video files. The user on the podcast platforms has to download these files in order to listen and view them. It follows the subscription model in which the new files added to the series are downloaded to the user's device automatically by the system. The name Podcast was suggested by Ben Hammersley, a British technologist, and journalist, by blending the words iPod and Broadcast. Mostly, audio and video files are found on the podcast platform, but few series also contain files in PDF and EPUB format.

Every person who generates a podcast uploads and maintains a list of files on the server which are accessed by the user only through the internet. In order to get updates related to the new files on the server, the user utilizes the podcatcher software on its device. Normally, the content on the podcast is high on volume. This is the main reason why experts rank it higher as compared to the normal broadcasting channels in terms of delivering the content to the targeted audience. Although broadcasting has more audience in terms of numbers, the podcast has the audience which is particularly interested in the content it offers. Moreover, podcasts can be listened to on-demand and at the will of the customer or user, not like broadcasting, which has a fixed schedule set by the operators.

Podcast, a Passive Income Source?

The answer to the question, "Is Podcast a source of passive income?" is, without a doubt, yes at any time. You just have to attain the right skills to create a podcast on a topic such as "How to improve yourself in music direction?". The skills and expertise are most important in the creation of an informative podcast that gets popular among the audience. Thereafter, it will become easier for you to utilize it in order to earn passive income on a regular basis from it. It is obvious that as a beginner, you have no idea how to use a Podcast for this purpose. But do not worry about this as we will guide you in this section to make it happen for you.

Podcast Sponsorships

You might not believe it, but some of the famous podcasts such as "The Art of Charm" earn billions of dollars through sponsorships on their content. The problem for many of the podcasters is to find a suitable sponsor. It can be done in three ways.

- Searching the advertisers by making use of your podcast.
- You start selling ad spots by your podcast.
- Just relax and produce quality content to attract advertisers to come to yourself.

The podcast sponsorship business idea follows the cost per impression model in which you will get,
- $18, if you manage to get 15000 downloads for 15-second payroll.
- $25, in case your podcast has 1000 downloads for 60-sec midroll.

Paid Books and Audiobooks

Normally, when you create a podcast, users get it free from through the podcatcher software on its device. People make use of your advice in their specific fields without even paying a single penny. Nonetheless, this situation can be changed if you manage to utilize content marketing in a smart way. When you create a guide in the form of books and audiobooks, make them very helpful for the users that they become ready to pay you for reading and listening to them.

Selling Branded Merchandise

In recent times, there are many examples found in the podcasting industry where fans support the podcaster by purchasing merchandise offered by it. The podcast can promote the brands and their products in order to generate revenue from their owners as well as through selling them. Moreover, Youtube also offers podcasters to place their content on its platform, along with the option of selling merchandise below the video. This enables the podcasters to place a link to the website or Shopify link of the product.

Advertising

The advertising revenue model can be utilized in the podcast platform, just like every other business. You can get passive income through placing ads of other companies and their products on your series of audio and video podcasts. In this way, your advertisers will pay you for a long time to promote their name. This means that it will result in an ideal passive income source if you manage to get sales in large numbers along with attracting large companies who are looking for promoting their product online.

Virtual Summits

The combination of podcasts and relationships can bring in great passive income for you. The only requirement is to make connections and relationships with the top experts who are also in the podcasting field. For organizing a virtual summit, you just have to combine interviews of these experts on different topics. The audience is generally eager to listen to these virtual summits on their topic of interest. After conducting the virtual summit, just put it on the digital platform and earn passive income through advertisement, paid charges, and sponsorships on your summit podcast.

Besides these options, you also have some other great tricks to generate profits from your well-created podcasts. The key is to build a podcast that attracts the larger audience and quality-wise it is good enough that they become ready to pay for purchasing it.

How to Create a Quality Podcast?

This topic is not completed until you learn or get an idea of how to create a podcast that has great content for the audience. The good thing in this field is that the hurdles to enter into it are low as compared to other businesses. Although it is simple to create a podcast, it's definitely tough to build a quality one. Take a look at the steps or tips you must have in your mind that are essential for this field.

1. Develop a concept for the podcast, which includes the name of the topic, length of the episode, and the format you are looking to upload on the host.
2. The next step is to design your artwork and the description of your podcast to advertise it to the audience.
3. Record and edit the podcast in the format you have selected. You will require the equipment according to the format, either video or audio you have chosen for the podcast.
4. Search out a platform to host your podcast. For example, you can host it on Libsyn and Podbean.
5. Lastly, do not forget to syndicate these files on the "RSS field," which makes them available on iTunes and also enables the user to download it on the device whenever it wants.

To conclude, the podcast industry is great for people with the right skills and knowledge to earn passive income. However, along with these skills, verbal communication is also very significant. Therefore, in order to try it out for generating a consistent passive income stream for yourself, make sure you fill all the prerequisites related to it.

CHAPTER 12
Car Rental

The car rental business is an idea which every one of you are aware of. This business is running across all the big cities of the world successfully for decades. The main operations of this business rely on renting a vehicle with a contract that lasts for a few hours, days, or at times goes on for weeks. Car rental agencies' main customers are those people who don't own their vehicle and require it for some time to travel within or out of the city's purpose. It is generally managed by the local branches located within the busy city areas.

Just like every business, with the time technology is impacting the working operations of the car rental business heavily. The convenience to rent a car is increasing for the customers, and the business growth is also witnessing an upward trend. For example, nowadays, customers can book their car for rent with online reservations through the website instead of visiting the local branch office of the company for this purpose. Besides this, car rental business companies are also adding new features to their service by using technology such as portable Wi-Fi or GPS navigation systems. However, it is predicted that technology has not fully taken over this business as its impacts will go further with time.

Car Renting and Passive Income

You may only be aware of only one aspect of the car renting business where you own a company and provide vehicles to the client on rent through it. In reality, the market has some stellar opportunities where you can earn great returns and passive income without making any hard effort. The options for car renting businesses are increasing with time, which are lucrative enough for you to start a side business along with your daily job and routine. You just have to analyze which market opportunity is suitable for you according to your financial position and working style. After that, all you have to do is relax and make a minimum effort to bring consistent cash flow in your bank account.

Rental Services

Let's start with the traditional car rental business idea where people rent out their cars to the customers for a variety of reasons. In recent times, this business option has new opportunities in the form of leisure car renting and business care renting. Many companies are in contract with car renting businesses to get the cars on rent basis for their working operations and providing vehicle facility to their executives. You just have to make sure that you are maintaining trendy and modern cars in your garage for business and leisure car renting business.

Car Leasing Services

This is one of the most desirable passive income ideas in the car renting business. In this method, you get into a contract with a customer as a car owner. The car leasing agreements are normally for a year or more in which you do not have to put any hard effort. Most of the clients of this service are large corporate companies whose employees are performing duties out of the city. It is a superb source of passive income through vehicle business where the car is leased out for a long period in which your part of work is no more than just the contract.

Sharing Services

It is a business idea that every serious minded entrepreneur can benefit from. Car sharing service business operates by pairing your car with a company that can find your clients who require a car for rent during the working days in your office time. Isn't it amazing to earn income passively even when you are performing duties at a regular job office? The passenger of the car pays the amount on a weekly or daily basis according to the contract mediated by the sharing services company. Hence, it makes a perfect choice for the people that do not have the financial capital and time for a startup business along with their regular job.

Party Bus Rental Business

It is another interesting and inspiring car rental business which does not have any significant competition right now. A party bus can also be referred to as a party ride that hosts ten or more people for recreational purposes. This is an innovative idea of business currently operated in countries like the United States, where people love to spend traveling holidays along with friends and family. The issue for this business funds for initial investment; otherwise, you just have to rent out the party bus for earning passive income.

Peer to Peer Car Sharing Companies

As we have discussed the impacts of technology on businesses all over the world, we will provide you an example of that here. There are many peers to peer car-sharing companies operating online. They offer car owners to rent out their cars by registering with them. They charged fees for providing clients and car maintenance services. In this way, you are able to relax in your home or regular job while consistent income in passive form is arriving in your account. The best example of such a company is Turo, which is operating in the USA.

Car Rental Industry Challenges

The above-discussed ideas are an attractive option for investors to start a side business for themselves. Yet, there are some challenges for the owners during the business operations, which they should be ready in advance. Here, you will find a list of top challenges a car rental business owner has to face and their solutions suggested by us.

Driving Challenges for Overseas Clients

Tourists and travelers from foreign countries are also major customers of the rental car business in many countries. Risks and chances of accidents with these clients are the highest. These clients are not familiar with the traffic rules and behavior of the visiting country. For this, it is ideal to provide a brief guideline regarding the traffic rules, roads, and routes before renting out the vehicle.

Managing Booking and Record

Record keeping and booking of the vehicles is the toughest task in the car rental business. The problem arises, especially when there are any price changes in the rents. Doing these tasks manually is not only hard, but there are plenty of chances for errors. The good news is that car management software is easily available at affordable rates to manage the daily operations and monitoring of the workers. This work can be monitored by you as a boss right from your home location.

Brand Awareness

 Renting field is not typically a reputation business where people are aware of the company benefits. People usually look to rent out the car from the nearest possible branch of any firm. Many of the old companies operate in big cities without any top exposure. Nonetheless, this situation can be changed, providing quality service, and doing digital marketing on social media platforms. Moreover, there should be a facility to the customers for car booking online through the website or mobile app.

New Technologies and Car Rental Business

The new companies in the market are entering with the updated technologies, which may be costly in nature. Older companies are facing tough competition due to the introduction of technology in the car renting business. Therefore, if you want to stay competitive in the car renting market, then it is advised that you should update your business regularly with the newer technologies available in the market.

Well, these challenges are tough to handle but are not impossible if you plan things right away. Most of these challenges are automatically dealt with when you follow our tips to earn passive income through the ideas we provided to you. Your focus should be on earning passive income rather than starting a business venture, which is your top priority all the time.

CHAPTER 13
Mobile App

Mobile applications are software programs that most of you are familiar with. These apps are developed to run on the smartphone on tablets. These apps contain limited functions and turn up the device into a powerhouse of features and fun. When you buy a smartphone, there are some built-in apps in its operating system. These apps are generally due to the courtesy of the manufacturers of the smartphone or tablet. In the era of technology, people are shifting from computers and PCs to handheld devices. These apps play an important role in the lives of people in a variety of ways.

The functions of these apps range from entertainment, fun, games, utility and productivity, and many others. Counting these functions is unimaginable for anyone in this world. However, social media apps are the top most used product either in iOS or Android world. Apps such as Facebook, Twitter, and Instagram are the most famous in this field. This indicates to the point that many of the websites have their app versions available to run on smartphones on a tablet. The reason behind this is that an app is much more interactive than the website and presents information in a way that is easy to run on the mobile.

Passive Income Through Mobile Apps

Let's get into our main topic, which is to discuss the ideas for generating passive income. Mobile apps are a great platform to earn passive income for the common people. You may get surprised by this statement. However, it is 100 percent true. Anyone having marketing knowledge can give you insight into how small companies are earning money through mobile apps. Apart from this, there are a number of other options where you can generate income with just a little effort.

App Ads

This is the prime source of revenue for all the categories of the apps. Mobile app developers and owners place ad ids on their apps. These ads are displayed to users by Google and iOS operating systems according to the ad strategy created by the app developer in the code. When a user clicks on the ad, the owner gets paid automatically. This way, the owners earn passive income by just making the app available for install on Google Play and iOS. The only requirement is to create a searchable app with attractive features, functions, and content to retain the user. You should also be familiar with the kind of app ads used by the developers and owners.

1.1.1. Interstitial Ad. This ad is displayed on the full screen of the app. This ad normally appears when someone is using the app.

1.1.2. Banner Ad. Typically displayed on a small area of the app screen while it is in usage.

The user clicks on these ads and visits the link of the related app whom the ad is showing. However, in the meanwhile, as an app owner, you are generating passive income into your account due to clicking on an ad displayed on your app.

In-app Purchase

Well, if you are a mobile game lover, then you should be familiar with this business model. In this idea, different mobile apps offer in-app purchases to install the pro-level of the app with more advanced functions. Moreover, game apps offer in-app purchases for playing high levels or offering new equipment for action games. Apart from this, if anyone is getting annoyed by the ads displayed on the app, they can get the ad-free version through in-app purchase. People pay for these in-app purchases and get the pro version. On the other hand, you are earning income from these payments while just relaxing and enjoying your daily life. Isn't it coon? Yes, it definitely is.

Lead Generation

In marketing, lead generation is a process where you can build interest or attract the customers towards the products and services of a brand or company. If you have an app on the Android Play Store, then you earn money by recommending the product of the other company from your app. In this way, the company you are providing leads to will pay you commission on their total sales. Apart from this, lead generation examples can be found in the form of selling data to other companies which are used for their business purposes. Mint.com is a perfect example of this app.

Transaction Fees

This business model involves high-level development and maintenance of the app. It may not be a passive income idea but allows you to earn income with less work. In these apps, financial transactions occur at a regular interval. The app is usually a sort of marketplace where the transaction of funds can be done just like crowdfunding. Your income generated by taking fees each time a transaction occurs using your app.

Subscriptions

Those mobile apps are based on content in the form of audio and video streams, online newspapers, or cloud services. The subscription process involves payment by the users to unlock certain features or sections related to the content of the app. For example, there is a 20-second promo of a video related to programming skills, but for full access users are asked to pay for it. In this way, the user will subscribe to the content, and you will get passive income into your account automatically without any hard effort.

To be able to generate cash flow from the mobile app through these models, you need to research an idea that is easily searchable and attractive for the users.

Best Passive Income Apps

This section will guide you towards the mobile apps that offer passive income. In the previous section, you read ideas on how to generate cash flow by developing your own app. However, now the focus is upon the apps that are a great passive income source by just simple usage. Most of the smartphone users are not aware of these income sources, but after reading the below points, you will surely will.

2.1. Swagbucks

Swagbucks is basically a survey app that also contains other features in it. Through this app, you have the chance to earn income by just watching ads, shopping online, and playing games on that app. Moreover, this app or site also provides income to your bank account if you make it as the default search engine on the web browser.

2.2. Panel App

This app rewards you with points if you share location data through your smartphone. This process is completed passively, and not even asks to use the app. The extra points can be earned through performing surveys and referring to a friend.

2.3. Drop Rewards

Drop rewards enable you to earn income in a unique way by registering your credit card on the app. All you have to do shopping at its recommended stores online, and in return, it will award you points. These points contain worth of 1 or 2 percent of the total purchases you make on these stores.

2.4. Savvy Connect
The main focus of the app is to find trending searches, entertainment stuff, and the content which most people like to see. By installing it on your phone, it will reward you with points at regular intervals according to the usage of mobile.

2.5. Dosh Rewards
It provides you income on the same credit card model, just like the Drop Rewards app. You have to shop online at stores and get paid back by earning rewards. This app is great for people with a large interest in buying items online rather than visiting the markets.

CHAPTER 14
Affiliate Marketing

Affiliate marketing is an advertisement based business model in which the company's products are promoted by a third party to earn the commission. The third-party basically refers to leads or customers to the company by advertising products or services through their platform. It is a great source of earning passive income in modern days. The third party is referred to be affiliated in this process who search the product they enjoy and then promote in their circle for earning commission on each sale.

It's based on a revenue sharing business strategy in which the owners of the product provide financial incentives to the advertisers in order to boost their sales. In the era of technology and the internet, the importance of affiliate marketing is growing day by day. This concept has been popularized by Amazon to the common public. Many bloggers and websites place the link of Amazon products on their page to divert the traffic to earn commission on sales. In short, affiliate marketing can be defined as a process which relies on a pay for performance business model in which the companies sell out their products through external sources.

How Does it Work?

The process of affiliate marketing involves various stages in which responsibilities are spread across different parties. It is a popular strategy to drive online sales and increase revenue by providing financial benefits to third party marketers. To make this process successful, there has to be involvement of the following parties in it.

- Product creators and service providers
- Affiliates or Marketers
- Customers

1.1. Product Creators/Service Providers
These are the individuals or companies whose role in the process is to be the seller or vendor of the products they create or the services they provide. The product is in physical form, and it can be any household items, clothes, materials, or anything else. The seller or vendor is not actively involved in the advertising process. Instead, it contracts with the affiliates to provide him leads. It gives commission or profit to the affiliates at every successful lead or at the visit of customers looking to purchase any product.

1.2. Affiliate

It can also be described as a publisher who promotes the product of the owner in an appealing way to the customers. For example, a blogger can place the link of the product on its website or by discussing briefly in its blogs. Moreover, many social media account owners earn income just by posting about the product or referring it to their followers.

1.3. Customers

Although the customers have no idea about this, they are the main drivers of the affiliate marketing process. Advertisers promote the product to them through blogs, social media, and websites. They are the ones who visit the link shared by advertisers and purchase the product on the owner's website. Through them, both product owners and affiliates earn income.

How to Start Affiliate Marketing as a Beginner?

For the successful launch of the affiliate marketing business, you must be aware of all the essentials involved in it. You should be aware of the stages involved in the process of creating an affiliate marketing platform in order to generate passive income from it. In this section, you will read the guideline on how to start affiliate marketing as a beginner.

2.1. Find Your Niche

Firstly, you need to be well informed about what niche is to identify the right one for you. It is a subset of a larger market such as tennis in the sports market. When you are looking for an entry in affiliate marketing, first research the niche that is suitable for you with less competitiveness so that you can easily target the audience. However, the niche must be large enough so that you are able to make profits from it. You can find the right niche through the following methods.

- Following current trends in the online world.
- Doing keyword research.
- Locate top influencers in the market.

2.2. Research Affiliate Programs

After selecting your niche, it's time to research the market for recognizing the programs and products to promote them. This process will take time; however, keep it in your mind that this is essential for earning passive income in the end. Your focus must be upon identifying what category of merchants is using the affiliate marketing in this niche. Moreover, get full knowledge about the product features to rightly promote it with your audience. In the end, calculate how much commission you can make from this market niche to decide whether you should finalize it or not.

2.3. Build a Platform

This is one of the crucial stages of setting up a passive income stream from the affiliate marketing field. You should be aware of the initial costs and struggle for getting success in this process. Building a platform means to develop a website with blogs and content, social media accounts, or mobile app where you can produce the company products to create leads. The company will pay you on each sale made through the audience you provide them through your platform.

2.4. Build an Audience

The next step is to build an audience on the platform you have chosen. For example, if you have selected Instagram for this purpose, then create quality posts to convince the audience to start following you. Besides the quality content, marketing and advertising are very critical to increasing loyal customers to your website, social media account, or mobile app. You can utilize search engine optimization for the website traffic as well as a paid advertising campaign in the form of PPC (Pay Per Click). The goal is to build an audience and followers enough so that you can advertise the product to generate a good number of leads for the company you are in contact with.

2.5. Promote Affiliate Offers

Lastly, the part that has the most important in affiliate marketing. Once you feel that you have the right number of audiences to promote the product, start showing them something of value. There can be different strategies used in this marketing process.

- Share real and honest reviews regarding the product of the company. The key is to build confidence among the audience, so they trust you in the future.
- Implement banner ads on your website or mobile to make the audience click on it, which will result in their visit to the product page.
- Place links within the content of the website or social media posts.
- Do email-marketing by first asking the audience to allow you for this.

Remember, the more you are able to divert traffic towards the product, the more you have chances to contribute towards the sale of the company.

Affiliate Marketing – a Great Source of Passive Income

The process is based on digital advertising of the product, if done properly, can turn out to be a steady stream of passive income. All you have to do is to share the link of the product through the content, ad placement, or post sharing from your platform. It requires the minimum effort in case you are running a website or mobile app. Nonetheless, you should not ignore the fact that in the beginning, you have to do some consistent hard work in the right direction to set up a suitable platform for this purpose.

It involves gaining or sharing the revenue without making any effort to manufacture or ship the product. You can choose between a one-time commission affiliation or a recurring commission model. It will increase your earnings even when you are sleeping or on vacation. For instance, once you have placed a banner ad on your website, then the visitors will keep clicking on it whenever they access the page. It can continue for a long time spanning years. In this way, you can earn income for a long time even after you have finished the work. Due to this, it is always beneficial to have it as an added income stream for any professional working in the digital marketing field. It can allow you to work on the weekends or in free time according to your will and then enjoy the passive income stream in the future.

As a fast and inexpensive way of adding passive income to the bank account makes affiliate marketing very popular among the public. However, you must also be well acknowledged by the methods it can add to the revenue stream apart from commission earned through sales. The affiliate can also be paid by the company for completing actions like signing up, contact form, or subscribing to an offer. Moreover, some companies also pay just for the pay per click process in which they just demand the insurance of visits by the consumer through your platform.

Just like all other home-based businesses, affiliate marketing also requires planning and hard work at the start. Although the probability of earning passive income through affiliate marketing is the same as other internet-based. Nevertheless, if you play the cards in the right direction, then it can prove to be a long-lasting source of income for yourself. The overall success of your affiliate marketing depends upon the execution of your plan.

CHAPTER 15
Dropshipping

Dropshipping is a business model that lets the owner-run its operation without maintaining a regular inventory or warehouse to store the products. Similarly, it is not your responsibility to ship the products to the customer residence or location. Once you have made a deal with the customer, or he/she purchases products from your page, then the purchased item will automatically be shipped by the supplier. In simple words, this business runs with the partnership between the retailer and the supplier. The supplier manufactures and ships the product to the retailer customer on its behalf with both of dividing the profit. Let's see the process of its working step by step below.

- The customer places the order from the page of the product managed by the retailer online.
- In the next step, the retailer forwards the request of the customer to the supplier with all the details required to ship the order.
- Supplier packages the product and then ships it to the customer location.

Isn't it cool for a person having no funds and place to set up an inventory for running the business? All you require is to have a laptop and a stable internet connection to proceed with the marketing operations and forwarding the request of the customer. The retailer has to manage customer complaints and inquiries regarding the product. It has no responsibility related to the manufacturing of the product. The retailer acts as a middleman or broker in this process. However, it sells the products of the supplier under his own name. Therefore, customers will complain to the retailer in case any issue arises.

Dropshipping turns out to be one of the most profitable and peaceful business choices available to you. The reason behind this that you are not responsible for the costs and hard work is done on the manufacturing, packaging, and shipping of the products. The income can be quickly earned in the passive form once you have to find the right suppliers. Therefore, it is a great way for yourself to become an entrepreneur during your free time at nights and weekends. The daily work required with processing order can be completed with just a number of clicks from your laptop.

Steps for Earning Passive Income Through Dropshipping

Since you have learned the basics of the dropshipping business, now it's time to learn how to set up it for earning a consistent income. The idea of creating a revenue stream without any physical involvement is no doubt attractive to everyone. In order to execute it at your home, read out the following tips which guide you step by step.

1.1. Research the Market and Products

As a new entry in the dropshipping business, your focus must be upon acquiring the customers and grabbing the market opportunity. Selecting the right product to sell through the dropshipping model has critical importance. You need to research what type of behavior and needs do your target market, and its demographics possess. This is essential for increasing the conversion rate when a customer visits your product page.

1.2. Locate the Supplier

As discussed earlier, major work in the dropshipping model is performed by the supplier. After you have selected the products to sell online as a retailer, now it's time to finalize the suppliers for the purpose of manufacturing, shipping, and packaging the product. Commonly, most dropshipping suppliers are available overseas. Therefore, do proper analyses regarding the communication and responsibility level your supplier possesses to complete the operations smoothly.

1.3. Build an ECommerce Website

To enable your customers to view and to order products online, there must be a web platform for an eCommerce website for this. Nowadays, anyone can build an online shop store website through WordPress. However, you can also take the services of a professional at low rates for this. Moreover, you also have the opportunity to launch a website through different eCommerce platforms available on the internet, such as Amazon and Shopify.

1.4. Marketing and Advertising

The most demanding aspect of this business model is to build an audience for your website and the products it offers. Therefore, you need to master digital marketing strategies, especially SEO and Pay per click campaigns. Moreover, you must also run social media ad-based campaigns as well as accounts to convert traffic to your website. Loyal customers cannot be attained without the proper marketing of your product in the digital business world today.

In the end, keep track of all the records through the data available to you. Maintain the lists regarding the orders you have forwarded to the supplier. To avoid any issues, make sure the communication between you and the supplier is regular and comfortable.

Advantages of Dropshipping Business and Passive Income

The convenience offered by the dropshipping business model has no comparison with other opportunities available in the business world. It has successfully attracted entrepreneurs from all over the world in recent years. Moreover, as a supplier, it also benefits you to get an increased number of orders without doing any marketing and advertising work. Besides, there are also some other advantages attached to dropshipping.

2.1. Minimum Risk
It involves minimum risk as a retailer since you have not spent the budget on inventory and warehousing. The only money you will lose if your business fails to capture the market is spent on marketing and building up an eCommerce website. Therefore, if the trends change, your business is at minimum risk to face the loss.

2.2. Easy Management of Variety of Products
Through your eCommerce website, you can offer a variety of products to the customers. You can get in contact with different suppliers depending upon the category of the products they offer. Correspondingly, all the hassle involved in shipping the product to different locations is carried out by the supplier.

2.3. Expansions in New Markets
When you are running a physical store with inventory and warehouse, then it becomes tough to explore new markets in different regions of the world. However, with dropshipping, you can market your product to newer markets without any concern on how to ship them at different locations. Your online website can be accessed by people all over the world to purchase the items.

CHAPTER 16
Freelance

A freelance career is exciting and lucrative for every professional in any field. It brings a lot of freedom and flexibility to work according to your own terms. Commonly, the start of a freelance career enables the professional to earn active income. It feels great to work to have the freedom to choose a project and work with your choice of clients. However, the issue arises when the professionals get overloaded with the burden of work. The reason behind this situation is the responsibility of all the tasks such as marketing, customer support, and research is upon you. It becomes tough to focus on your work with these activities.

However, when you have set up multiple income streams with high rates, then it can provide you room to earn passive income with reasonable profits. Keep it in your mind that generating passive income is a lot tougher in the start then to earn active income as a freelancer. Nonetheless, if you play your cards right, then all you have to do is just monitor the passive cash flow roll in. The market has the potential to provide you with a number of opportunities to generate passive income depending upon the field you are working on and the skills you have. Therefore, stop trading your daily time to earn dollars and work smartly to earn passive income. Here are our recommendations to convert your freelance career into a passive income stream, which provides you consistent profits without any considerable hard work.

Outsourcing Your Projects

For building up a network to generate passive income, you are required to take some time away from a freelance working career. The best strategy to find time for passive income is to outsource your current and future projects. There are a number of freelance workers available on Fiverr, Freelancer, and Upwork platforms whom you can hire to complete the work. If you are unable to find a suitable worker for your whole project, then at least outsource the major part of your project. This will provide you enough time to get in touch with multiple clients and grow your network to earn passive income by forwarding the projects.

Identify a Niche

Research and analyze your skills to select a niche where you can satisfy the audience for taking the projects. This does not mean that your clients will take information from you regarding the field. You have to provide a solution and the working strategy to make them realize that you are perfect for this job. After acquiring the project, just forward it to any freelance worker available on the internet to earn profits.

Selling Unused Work

At times, freelancers end up with the work that cannot be termed as complete or meeting with the requirements. However, this work can also be sold to people online. Whether it is a written code, graphic design, or images, there are many potential buyers for this stuff who make use of it in their projects. However, make sure that the content you are selling is legally owned by you or purchased earlier from the owner in the first part.

Flip Websites

The common public with no understanding of the programming or website creation can be ideal customers for freelancers. They are ready to pay huge money for the already created or running websites and blogs. It's like flipping in a home where you build up the website and then sell it at a high rate. Moreover, such clients are also willing to pay you money for maintaining the websites. Therefore, it is recommended to be a great source of passive income if you know how to build up the website.

Refer Work for Commissions

Another smart way to earn passive income is to get in collaboration with professionals in different fields. Your job is to refer them to a client or work and, in return, get a commission on the total fee of the job. In this way, it will be flexible for you to just communicate the information between the client and professional to bring in cash to your account. All you have to do is to get in touch with the clients on different platforms online and inquire them what services they require. It acts a bit like network marketing where you refer to the company through the code to earn passive income.

Sell Work

As a freelance worker, you have the option to build stuff to sell it online by yourself. For instance, if you have excellent writing skills, then you can write a book and sell it on kindle publishing. Correspondingly, freelancers can get the work done from other professionals to create templates, designs, apps, and invoices to sell them online. Besides this, you can also use subscription and sponsor models to earn passive income by working only one time and then sell the work for a long period.

When you are looking to earn passive income as a freelancer, then keep it in mind that you have to face some serious challenges at times. For example, when you are outsourcing a project, you may have problems meeting the deadline. This can happen if the worker you have hired has some issues or less capacity and skills to complete the job on time. Moreover, both passive and active income earned by freelance work involves no insurance and health benefits by the companies you provide services too. Nonetheless, the flexibility and convenience offered by the freelance business strategy is a great attraction for people looking to earn both passive and active income. Sometimes, it may require months of work in the start to bring in some fruits for your efforts, but when the right strategy clicks, then cash flow comes into your account on a consistent basis.

CHAPTER 17
Bike Rental Business

Nowadays, many billion-dollar businesses don't even host an asset to operate their functions. Yes, it's true whether you believe it or not. For instance, Airbnb and Uber are running their worldwide business by providing marketing places to third party facilitators and customers. Therefore, it can rightly have said that it is the beginning of a new era in the business world where the pressure of ownership has reduced very much. Correspondingly, the world is moving towards renting assets for businesses which have given rise to a number of opportunities for entrepreneurs to take advantage of earning passive income.

Renting a bike business can be a useful business option to generate passive income for yourself. This won't make you rich or impact the bank balance quickly but can provide you a reasonable income to cover some expenses of your life. People living in urban cities look to rent out the bikes of roaming around the city on a daily basis. It creates an opportunity to run a side business for you in which less hard work is required. The growing trend of renting a bike business in large cities all over the world validates the idea that this business can provide you commercial benefits. The bike can generate your passive income with just you need to keep it in good shape to satisfy the consumer's mind.

People are looking to rent out anything extra present in their home. Whether it is a vehicle or extra rooms through the online marketplaces. This creates the space to provide alternative transport options such as bikes to the consumers who are looking for cheap traveling options. In the technology world, many companies are providing you platforms to share your bike for rent. This option reduces the workload to a minimum as these companies are providing your customers without any hard work required by your side. We will look at these startup companies that create opportunities for earning passive income through renting a bike to the customers. Moreover, we will provide you the guidelines on how to use these platforms for your side business.

Tips for Increasing Profits by Renting a Bike

Every business looks to improve its products and services for increasing the profit and income they are gaining from it. If you want to start a bike renting company or startup, then you are advised to go through the following sections to smartly improve the profit you earn from it.

1.1.Excellent Listing

When you are running a bike renting business, focus on the target market this business has. Your customers are aiming to hire a bike for having a blast or fun all around the city most of the time. Therefore, you must maintain a great listing of the bike in your store or showroom.

1.2. Keep Gear
When you are offering bikes for renting, there are high chances that your customers won't have the necessary products, such as a helmet to drive the bike. Maintaining a cheap gear would result in attraction for customers as well as a side option for earning higher fees for rent.

1.3.Strategic Pricing
Setting the price for renting the bike is critical for the success of your business and earning passive income. Make sure you analyze the price settled by the competitors. Always try to settle for the price that is attractive for the customer to choose your company over the others.

1.4. Buy Bikes Popular with Consumers
Purchase cheap bikes but those with fewer maintenance requirements and have low insurance costs. Some of the popular bikes among the renters these days are Ducati monsters and Adventure Bikes. Since you are purchasing it for rental business, then reach out for the cheaper and older versions available in the market.

How to Advertise Bike Rental Company

The marketing and advertisement of business are critical to success. Despite the fact that the bike renting demand is ever-increasing still, there are many companies that are not making enough profits. The reason can be poor advertisement and failure in creating awareness among the masses.

2.1. Search Engine Optimization
Most people search online regarding the rental companies operating their city. Therefore, make sure that your website is ranked top of the list when a user makes a search on Google and Yahoo search engines. For this, you have to perform keyword research and then utilize them smartly in the content and URL of the website.

2.2. Social Media Marketing
In the last decade, social media has become the most powerful tool for creating awareness among the public related to anything. You need to utilize this platform to aware people regarding your company in the city

it is based in. Most customers of bike rental companies are based, and residents of that specific city. Therefore, target social media users according to the location of the company.

2.3. Co-brand with Businesses

Co-branding is a very useful marketing strategy for startup companies. It brings exposure to the customers of the co-brand. Moreover, a new company can also take advantage of the positive image of the other brand. The best option for bike renting companies is to get in touch with the tourist companies to advertise the bike rental companies. These tourist companies will bring you customers that love to travel within and out of the city.

2.4. Follow up with emails

Following up with your target audience can prove to be effective in the bike rental business. It is ideal to send promotional emails to your customers right after they have returned the bike. Customers can be attracted by the invitation to fill performance feedback to make them realize that their opinion matters to your management.

The focus should be to devise a marketing strategy that meets customer demand. You must do research on what people are looking for while renting a bike from the company. Overall, the bike renting business is growing with time and is a great source for generating passive income for you. However, the problems should be dealt with seriously, and proper planning must be done in order to develop a successful passive income stream.

CHAPTER 18
Sell Photos And Videos

The concept of passive income attracts everyone in the world. It is a great feeling to sit back and let the cash flow in your account on a consistent basis. This excitement can go to another extent if you can integrate your passion with the professional life that brings you passive income for a long time. Just imagine you are taking photos of nature and making videos because of your passion and then selling it online for earning money. Every passive income stream requires hard work at the start and some consistent input from the business owner to keep the passive cash flow arriving in the account. However, when you turn your passion for photography into a business, then the burden of hard work can be mentally tackled easily due to love for the work and field.

How to Earn Passive Income From Photos and Videos?

The problem is most people don't have the idea of how to profit from their passion for photography. Generally, people think that the only way to create income from photography is to search out the clients and then do a photo session with them. However, in reality, there are a number of ways you can earn money in a passive way, especially for those who do not want to be an event photographer. In this section, we will guide you on quality ideas and business strategies to build a passive income stream by selling photos and videos.

1.1. Sell Photos and Videos at Stock Photo Site

Stock photography is an interesting business strategy to sell intellectual property rights and legally use videos and photos. This can be one of the most useful methods to earn passive income online. The process is very simple in which you, as a seller, sign up as a contributor and upload your stock on these websites. If anyone likes your photos and videos and wants to utilize it on their website or any other place, they will pay you for that. Just market your work and get the passive income in your account.

1.2. Use Multiple Websites

This may seem simple to you but requires deep research work to find out the websites where you can place your work for selling it online. The priority must be to utilize multiple websites in order to spread your content to a larger section of the audience. In our next section, we will refer you to some useful websites that can help you find clients to purchase your photos and videos.

1.3. Refer Others to Earn Commissions

When you get into the business, make sure you bring all the innovative strategies to increase your revenue. As a photography passionate, you surely have a network of people that love photography. This creates an opportunity to earn passive income by referring them to purchase videos and photos on websites like Shutterstock. In the end, you will earn a commission on each sale made based on your referral.

1.4. Create Your Own Website

Working on the model of affiliate marketing, you can advertise your stocked photos through your own website. For example, if you run a blog, then you can place a link of your stocked photos and videos to divert traffic on that page. This can be beneficial to increase your visiting audience. Moreover, it can also provide you with room to start an affiliate marketing business strategy to earn passive income.

1.5. Target Niche Market

This means creating content by targeting a specific market niche. Many websites and blogs are looking for photos to place on their articles online. For example, you can create a collection related to teaching and school learning, which cannot be found easily for free. The bloggers will simply pay you for the content they want to legally use it at their website. However, the key is to understand the demands of niche marketing and proper research work on how many clients are available for this field.

Recommended Platforms to Sell Photos and Videos

As a newcomer, you might not have any idea on how to sell your photos and videos online using different channels. Here, we will recommend some of the best platforms where you can earn passive income selling your work to the clients. Take a look at them one by one.

2.1. Adobe Stock

It is a stock photo market created by popular image editing platforms Photoshop and Lightroom. It is known to be the first platform to be run on this business idea. The photos added to it are included in the library and are available in different adobe applications such as Photoshop. This means larger access to the audience and clients.

2.2. Shutterstock

Probably, the most popular online marketplace to sell and purchase images, videos, and music royalty-free. They have millions of customers who can bring you a lot of revenue passively. They also offer you to keep the copyrights while selling the videos and photos. When a user downloads any video or photo, you as a contributor are paid automatically on a monthly basis.

2.3. Alamy
It is another useful platform to sell your photography work online to earn passive income. They pay you 50 percent of the selling price, which is a great attraction for commercial photographers. Furthermore, it does not create any issues related to licensing copyrights when you upload photos and videos.

2.4. Fotomoto
Fotomoto is also an online marketplace that operates with a widget that integrates with photos and videos placed on your own website. You have to add it to the site, and then it further handles the process itself to sell your photos and videos. It includes multiple plans related to fees charged by it for services. Isn't it great to just add the widget and then relax while cash coming to your account consistently?

2.5. PhotoShelter
An online platform that allows you to deliver prints and photos and your clients if any order is made. It allows you to build templates to attract customers to purchase your work. The notable thing is that you have to pay for getting space on the platform to place your work for selling.

To conclude this section, selling photos and videos has become a great source for generating cash flow with the advent of online marketplaces. The demand for unique pictures and videos related to the different fields is on the rise. The reason behind this is the online representation of every business and information blog. Overall, it is a great opportunity for photography lovers to turn their passion into a proper career for life.

CHAPTER 19
Create Online Courses

People use the internet for a number of reasons with entertainment and socializing at the top of the list. However, the internet is also utilized for learning purposes and to explore knowledge and information. The Internet is full of guidelines and tutorials to do almost everything possible in this universe. For instance, if you are having issues with any feature of window OS, then there must be a tutorial on how to fix the problem or guideline on how to use the features on YouTube. Similarly, each life activity has been discussed on the internet, such as preparing dinner, computer learning, sports techniques, or diet plans. These are just examples; in reality, literally, everything is available to get guidance from the internet.

As people are getting more familiar with technology, the understanding of using the internet for productive purposes is also increasing. People are searching for solutions to their daily life problems more and more on the internet. Correspondingly, many students are finding it flexible to go for e-learning instead of attending academies for learning purposes. For instance, if an IT graduate wants to sharpen his/her skills in Java Development, then he/she just has to search the internet to get online courses available. This convenience has increased the interest of common people, which is the main reason for the growing need for learning things online.

In this scenario, experts in different fields have great opportunities to create income up learning and guide courses online. Many people misunderstand this process as they think expertise is required for creating an online course. This isn't the case; in reality, you are just required to know more than most of the people. Apart from this, you must have good communication skills to clearly guide the learners about the topic. You have the choice to create online courses in a variety of topics, from technical to household activities as well as educational studies.

Tips to Create Online Course

As a beginner, you must focus on basics and completely understand the tips to create the online course. You need to perform different tasks as it requires more than just knowledge in a particular domain. The second stage of creating an online course is how to generate passive income from it. First, focus on what you should consider in order to create an effective online course.

1.1. Decide Should I Create Courses?

Before you start working hard for creating an online course, it's better you analyze whether you should do it or not? For this, consider the following points and make decisions on that basis.

- Do I have enough knowledge or expertise in any specific field?
- Does my area of knowledge have an audience or not?
- Is my schedule providing me time to create a course without any issue?
- Am I ready to do marketing for creating awareness among the public?
  If the answer is "Yes" to all the above questions, then go for it otherwise rethink it.

Market Research

As you have decided that you have enough knowledge and skills to create the course in a specific field in the above step, now it's time to do some market research. Try to find out what people are looking to learn online in your field. For example, in digital marketing, there are various topics, so search the most demanded one, such as Search Engine Optimization.

Create Your Lessons

Next, start creating your tutorials or series of videos or audios for online. You need to consider two things in it.

- Outline the course
- Select a method to deliver lessons.
- Creation of the course according to the method selected.
- Proofreading or quality check.

Online Course Software

The next step in creating an online course for passive income is to choose a hosting platform to make sure it is available for the users. Commonly, there are three options available to you to host your online course.

Course Marketplace. This is the most convenient way to build up a course and start selling it to the clients. You just have to sign up and then build up the course on the marketplace. The disadvantage these marketplaces have that they charge you fees at each purchase made by the client. The most popular marketplaces for online courses are Udemy and SkillShare.

Hosted Platform. In this hosting method, you pay the fee once or monthly rather than giving commission to the website on each sale. The course does not have any support regarding the marketing from such marketplaces. The top examples of such marketplaces are ZippyCourses and Teachable.

Self-hosted Course. The self-hosted course isn't a bad option for you if you are willing to put some extra effort into it at the start. You can market the course yourself with only one-time payment on attaining hosting rights. You can take the services of a professional developer for creating a stunning website for your online course.

How to Generate Passive Income From Online Course

Once you have created the course and placed it on a hosting platform, now it's time to generate passive income through it. It involves strong marketing and advertising at the start, but if you play all the cards right, then you can earn money on a consistent basis with just a little effort. You have to perform the following actions to make your online course profitable for you.

- Offer paid courses to the students and clients with proper advertising that how beneficial the course will be for them.
- Make the course free to view or take but charge for getting certification by your company.
- Use the subscription model as we have discussed in various other sections in the book.
- Sell courses and its license to other companies who are doing this business. They will take care of marketing and technical problems as their own.
- Implement a tiered payment system where premium sections in your course require payment to proceed.

In the end, you are advised to share whatever you know well as people are hungry to learn new things in life. It can be a great business option for you if you can build a strong reputation for your course.

CHAPTER 20
Create A Lifestyle Blog

Writing about yourself and life experiences continue to flourish even in the modern era. We have just replaced the pen and paper with a laptop or tablet to take the memory of our experiences. Furthermore, there are other options also surfaced on the scene like Vlog to share your life happenings with others in video form. However, since our topic is creating a blog of our own experiences, therefore, we will stay on the topic of writing about our life. This is a unique way of attracting visitors to your website as people are always conscious of reading what's happening in other's lives and how they deal with situations, problems, and opportunities.

The goal is to not only share your life stories with others but to make it profitable for you in terms of financial purposes. Besides this, your own blog makes you feel comfortable to work flexibility and work with independence. Therefore, you can write anything you want to share about your life or thoughts about any process around you. However, keep the audience taste in mind and provide something interesting to them with a consistent flow to make loyal readers of your blog. After that, you have to utilize some standard marketing and tactics to generate passive income from your blogs. The personal experiences you write in the form of the blog will stay on your website forever, and people will come up to read them, which will create opportunities for you to earn money even after many years.

The focus of our section is to provide you suggestions that are critical to creating a personal blog based on your experiences that will help you make a loyal audience. If you write things in the right way, then it can be great for your bank balance as blogs with high traffic earn an immense amount of income passively. Take a look at these tips or suggestions below.

Basic Structure

In any blog post, the basic structure must be in unity and harmony to present the work in a professional way. Ideally, the basic structure of your must be:

- Start with an introduction to catch the user's attention instantly.
- Next, write up the main body, where you explain everything to the reader.
- This is the review of everything you discussed in the above sections of the post.

Connected Paragraphs

Focus on writing paragraphs of the blog post, which seems to be in one flow. Each paragraph can have its own topic, but it should be interlinked with the main topic of your personal experience or story.

Style of Personal Experience

These types of blogs are observed to be successful when they are written in an informal style. Make sure you are writing as if you are talking to someone. Just imagine you are telling a story to your friend. Similarly, do not try to be a specialist writer and just focus on bringing your personality out of the blog post. The reader should have a sense that he/she is listening to a story from someone he/she has a deep relationship with.

Be Truthful

Feelings have no connection with the whole process of blogging. Just express your emotions on your blog regarding the incident or situation you are presenting a story or thoughts about. Remember, you are not writing up the blog to make people happy. Your first goal is to share your own experience with others. Being truthful about things will also help you to discover new things in your own personality.

Research Niche

Although you are running a blog to share your life experiences with the readers. However, you cannot drive huge traffic to your website without doing proper market research on what people like to read. Therefore, if you are looking to generate passive income through your personal experiences blog, then share the stories of your life which people are most interested in. The top areas which most visitors like to read about other's experiences are:

- Travelling and tourism experiences of one's life at different locations
- Health problems and how you overcome them.
- Life career challenges and struggle stories.
- Bloggers can share their emotional breakouts and how life was tough for them in the past.
- Gaming and Tech blogs and Vlogs are getting very popular these days.
- Parental stories regarding their family development and childcare.

Running a blog of your personal experiences can be an exciting business idea. If you have an interest in sharing your stories with others, then it will not have mentally tiring impacts. The key is to build up the blog in such a way that you get enough traffic on it. This goal of attaining traffic or visitors is critical for monetizing your blog. You can implement advertisements, affiliate marketing, sell products, and do marketing for other companies through it to generate passive income. We have discussed the above techniques to earn passive income in the corresponding sections of the book.

CHAPTER 21
Create A Shopify Store

Shopify is one of the most inclusive online e-commerce platforms where you can sell products to customers through developing your own website or online store. It charges you on a monthly basis to create an online store for the purpose of promoting, selling, and shipping products. They provide you admin access where you can add products, list them, and process different orders through it. Anyone can build a promising online store by using themes present on the Shopify platform. Therefore, it can be said that Shopify is the easiest and most simple way to sell products to the worldwide market by merchants and entrepreneurs.

Choosing a Plan

Though you get a 14-day free trial, you need to think long term. Which pricing plan fits your goals the best? Shopify offers a $9/month Point of Sale, henceforth shortened to POS, only stores with no online shop, but if you are reading this, you are probably interested in at least a small online presence.

It is important to note that any pricing plan comes with a few core features. You can have any number of products for sale. If you want to sell anything and everything, while I would not recommend this, you definitely can. All plans come with Shopify POS, meaning you can sell in person and collect payments through an app on your phone.

All the online store pricing plans, starting at $29/month, come with unlimited bandwidth and storage, meaning you will not be charged extra based on the number of viewers or customers and you can upload all the photos you need to give those customers the best idea of what they are buying. They also come with all available sales channels. These include, but are not limited to, Amazon, Facebook, and a "buy button" you can place on your own website. You also get fraud analysis to ensure you are getting paid.

On the customer's end, you can send discount codes for various occasions, such as getting new customers or post the codes to your social media. You can also customize the "Abandoned Cart Recovery" (ACR) email that is sent to users when they leave the store without completing the checkout process.

Shopify Lite- $9/month

This is the cheapest plan but removes your online store. You do still, however, get the "Buy Button" and the ability to sell on Facebook or in person with POS.

Basic Shopify- $29/month
This plan gives you all the basics in addition to an online store. It allows two staff accounts and four locations to track and fill orders from. It has card rates of (2.9% + $0.30) online or 2.7% in person. You also get a slight discount when printing shipping labels from Shopify.

Shopify- $79/month
This is the most popular because it adds gift cards and brings the total to 5 staff accounts and 5 locations. You also get a better discount on printed shipping labels and a credit card rate of (2.6% + $0.30) online and 2.5% in person.

Advanced Shopify- $299/month
This is the best offer Shopify has. It offers shipping rates calculated by a third party and brings the best discount on printed shipping labels. It also gives a grand total of 15 staff accounts and 8 locations. The credit card rates are (2.4% + $0.30) online and 2.4% in person.

Shopify Lite- $9/month
This is the cheapest plan but removes your online store. You do still, however, get the "Buy Button" and the ability to sell on Facebook or in person with POS.

Basic Shopify- $29/month
This plan gives you all the basics in addition to an online store. It allows two staff accounts and four locations to track and fill orders from. It has card rates of (2.9% + $0.30) online or 2.7% in person. You also get a slight discount when printing shipping labels from Shopify.

Shopify- $79/month
This is the most popular because it adds gift cards and brings the total to 5 staff accounts and 5 locations. You also get a better discount on printed shipping labels and a credit card rate of (2.6% + $0.30) online and 2.5% in person.

Advanced Shopify- $299/month
This is the best offer Shopify has. It offers shipping rates calculated by a third party and brings the best discount on printed shipping labels. It also gives a grand total of 15 staff accounts and 8 locations. The credit card rates are (2.4% + $0.30) online and 2.4% in person.

Setting Up

Before we can jump to products and inventory, you need to input some information about your store. Log in and make sure to temporarily password-protect your store. This allows you to test out the bugs and features before putting your store out to the public. Then, you do some of the basics. Name your store; choose your store's legal business name and address; add your billing information; set the defaults for currency and weight; set up the domain; get staff members if necessary.

We will cover choosing products and gaining inventory in later chapters, but you would generally place a couple of products as a test in this stage. We will also cover metadata and promotion in later chapters, but it is best to get these down quickly, as it will allow people to find your store easier.

Testing and Troubleshooting

To make sure everything will run smoothly, add a couple of test orders, and test the following things:

- Successful and failed transactions
- Canceling orders
- Refunds
- Completing or partially filling orders
- Archiving your successful transactions

After you have done all the troubleshooting, you're ready to remove the password and give access to everyone on the world wide web.

Other Sales Channels

You may recall earlier when I mentioned sales channels offered with any Shopify plan. These are all highly recommended as they present your store to wider audiences.

If you have a personal website or blog, you may add a Buy Button for some of your most popular products with a link to your Shopify store.

You can also use other sites like Pinterest, Facebook, Etsy, Amazon, or even Facebook Messenger.

How Does it Operate?

The process of Shopify is a step by step process to set up an online store where you have the technical support by the platform itself. In order to become an online merchant with Shopify, you have to go through the following process.

- Start with signing up on the Shopify website. This step will require you to fulfill your personal details as well as the store name. Moreover, you have to choose a membership plan for Shopify, which is recommended to be "Free Trial" at the start.
- Set up your store after signing up on Shopify. You will have to upload products, payment, and shipping methods. Furthermore, choose the theme of your store interface from the list provided by Shopify.
- After that, add the products you want to sell on your online store. You have the option to add collections in the form of categories and deals. The processing of adding products will require you to add name, description, and URL.
- Fill in your tax payment details and product delivery method. You have the option to set the shipping rates in the settings. You can adjust the rates according to weight or location.
- Moving on, make your website go live. This will require a domain name and hosting. Fortunately, Shopify also offers you to purchase the domain hosting from itself. This will be added to your store website automatically. Besides this, you can also purchase domain hosting from the third party. However, in this method, you will require some effort to redirect DNS records, which can be hectic.

The domain adding is the last step in getting your store ready at Shopify. In order to market your products, SEO techniques and blogs can be added to increase the number of visitors at your store.

Integrating Apps With Shopify

As an owner of the online store at Shopify, you can earn profits through your sale. However, it will require hard work from you to manage inventory, stores, and shipping. This effort has to be done if you are taking responsibility for everything regarding the products you are selling. However, there is another option available too. In the last section of this chapter, we have described the Dropshipping method for earning passive income. The good news is that Shopify offers you to integrate Dropshipping apps from where you can acquire the products. This will end up all the hard work and stress on you related to manufacturing, packaging, and shipping of the product to customer location.
The Shopify marketplace provides you the opportunity to add Dropshipping apps at any time. There is a number of Dropshipping available to you, which we will recommend later that which one is best for you according to category. The addition of the Dropshipping module

will let you set up a passive income stream through Shopify online store. Here, we will guide you on how to add a Dropshipping app to your online store. Mostly, the procedure followed by all these apps the same at Shopify. Take a look at this step by step process below.

- Start by clicking on the "Apps" button from the sidebar in the admin section.
- This will open up the list of top apps trending in the market. If you cannot find the desired app, then click on the " Visit the Shopify App Store" button to find it.
- Open the app details page by clicking on its name. Read the details and specifications of the app. Click on the " Add App" button in order to install it on Shopify online store or website.
- You will be required to the web address of the online store in some cases. Nonetheless, a pop-up screen will appear with information on what this app will do to your account. If you are satisfied with it, then click the "Install App" button.
- Select the products you want to sell from the app you have selected.

It is a very simple procedure to add the Dropshipping app but requires strong research work to select the right products that can actually sell.

How to Select Shopify Dropshipping Apps

The choice of dropshipping app is critical for the success of Shopify's passive income business. The reason is each app has different dimensions and quality. If you get connected to a wrong supplier or app, then the business can witness a tremendous downward trend. Therefore, you must be careful when adding dropshipping apps to your online store in order to offer products to the customers. You must need to check the following points and merits of a dropshipping app when choosing it for your online store.

- Best quality drop shipping available lets you choose the products from the Shopify platform or perform quick sync of your selected products to the store.
- Add the apps that are backed by quality suppliers. This can be done through research; however, quick options are to check reviews and ratings to get the idea.
- The Shopify store, at times, has issues with the shipping time. Therefore, choose the app which has suppliers present all around

the world. The problem can arise if you are a merchant from the USA, and the app you choose has all suppliers from Asia.

- Has the customer care record of the app satisfactory or good? This question must be in your mind while selecting the app.
- Look for the app that offers you product samples. This will ensure quality and customer satisfaction. Hence, it will be beneficial for an increase in your sales.
- You should check the apps that offer custom branding to the Shopify stores. For example, if a customer buys a product from your store but receives it from the brand name of the dropshipping app, then it can be confusing and lose credibility. Therefore, add your Shopify store name as a brand on it.

Top Dropshipping Apps on Shopify

As you are ready to select the right dropshipping app, now we will recommend to you some of the best apps available on the Shopify marketplace. This section will help you in choosing these apps according to the store category you own and the products you are planning to sell. Take a look at the below table, which contains the list of the dropshipping apps and when to choose them for online stores.

Dropshipping App	Reason for Selection
1. Oberlo	Choose it when you are planning to sell items. This app has a supplier group from all regions of the world. It provides an automatic update to the product availability in your store.
2. Spocket	If your target market is the USA and Europe, then Spocket is the best choice for the online store. Spocket offers a 45 percent discount to the merchants, leaving enough opportunity for earning profits.
3. Modalyst	It offers a brand name to the online store it gets product orders from. Make it your top choice if you have the priority to sell products under your own brand name.
4. Printiful	Select this app for products if you are looking to add print on demand goods to the Shopify online store.

	It also has suppliers from different regions of the world.
5. Spreader	Planning for affiliate marketing on Amazon products then add Spreader to your store. This gives you an analysis to choose the products from Amazon that are trending.

In the end, we are hoping that you are ready to take a chance with Shopify's online store to earn passive income. Be careful with your choices so that there is consistent cash flow coming in your bank account in passive form.

DESCRIPTION

The book of passive income that you are holding reveals all the secrets of earning passive income. By keeping the key points in mind about individuals who are looking forward to earning income through passive routes. Those who got tired of their daily life jobs want to spend their struggle of daily routine and wish to earn passively, but do not have their mindset about how they can start it or which online business suits them best. If you are also struggling with these questions, then you have the right solution in your hands. This book has specially designed for your readers who want to earn smartly and enjoy passive earnings

In this book, we have included all the basic steps to start your own online business. We have also focused on this book about the costs of starting your business and even provided you the idea of income that you can earn through this. When you are going to read this book, you will be able to clear your every single doubt of having an online business. When you move ahead in reading this book you will find the top most online business ideas from which you can choose the idea that suits you the best. If you feel tired from your daily job but don't have the mindset to start an online business because of your fear of failure, this book will serve as an aid for you. In this book, we have taken into consideration the mindset to succeed. Reveals to you how you can set your mind to achieve success. This book will prove to be the best solution for all your queries of passive income. In this book, we have put some inspiring stories of successful entrepreneurs who have successfully adopted the online business idea and earned handsome figures from these online businesses.

When you read their success stories, you will self-feel inspired to start your own.

This book is specially designed by keeping people in mind and reveals all the successful pathways of passive income. In this book, you also find some amazing key steps to generate passive income, which will guide you to start your own online business.

We have covered to an extent all the secrets, especially the way of generating passive income through blogging, affiliate marketing, Amazon FBA, online courses, kindle publishing, etc. We not only explained the steps only but also explained their benefits and other related aspects that will help you in guiding in a pure sense.

We have included suitable examples of successful entrepreneurs to take you close to the concept of this book. If you are looking for a solution for passive income in a book, then this book is specially designed for your readers. You will not only enjoy this book, but also you will feel inspired by this book. This book aims to take you close to the secrets of passive income. In this book, you will also find tricks and tips to solve the common problems that you face when you are going to start an online business. This book is a pure solution to your questions. Without any doubt, you can have this book and make yourself familiar with all the keys of passive income. Last but not least, if you are interested, just grab this book in your hand.

Lightning Source UK Ltd.
Milton Keynes UK
UKHW022038291222
414611UK00003B/21